Rice

NIKKY FINNEY

Rice

poems

Foreword by Kwame Dawes

TRIQUARTERLY BOOKS/NORTHWESTERN UNIVERSITY PRESS
EVANSTON, ILLINOIS

TriQuarterly Books
Northwestern University Press
www.nupress.northwestern.edu

Printed in the United States of America

10   9   8   7   6   5   4   3   2   1

Library of Congress Cataloging-in-Publication Data
Finney, Nikky.
    Rice : poems / Nikky Finney ; foreword by Kwame Dawes.
       p. cm.
    "First edition copyright © 1995 by Lynn Carol Nikky Finney. First published in Toronto (Ontario, Canada) in paperback in 1995 by Sister Vision: Black Women and Women of Colour Press."
    Includes bibliographical references and index.
    ISBN 978-0-8101-5232-8 (pbk. : alk. paper)
    1. South Carolina—Poetry. 2. African Americans—South Carolina—Poetry. I. Dawes, Kwame Senu Neville, 1962– II. Title.
PS3556.I53R53 2013
811.54—dc23
                                                                                    2013004308

For

Frances Davenport Finney, Newberry girl,

and Ernest Adolphus Finney Jr., Smithfield boy,

for

raising me in the country of your love

CONTENTS

Winnow

Kwame Dawes

Dear Nikky,

There is little else I can do but respond to your collection, which, I confess, was clandestinely acquired and which I read with the furtive excitement of a child who is reading taboo—actually in print. The collection produces a feeling—a sense of confidence that allows the complex to become distilled into simple wisdom. Very often, your poems assume that quality of clarity and directness that one associates with prophetic utterances or the sagelike wisdom of grandpeople:

> All along the ocean's floor
> There are attics
> And storm cellars of hearts
> Castanetting for a key
>
> Tell them I am on my way
>
> I am a woman with keys
> Unlocking all the buildings
> That now belong
> To me

The quality is "herstorical"—it represents an act of salvaging, an assertion of a positive voice that is oracular even if soft on irony and self-deprecation. It is a quality that is not easy to achieve. Many of us simply hide behind irony and witticism because we feel awkward when we attempt to sound like truth sayers. You cut through this and yet emerge a poet—a voice that is resonant with imagery and guile. All this accomplished while you still succeed in allowing the truths to float on a wave of musicality.

The Western tradition of the past two hundred years has entailed the gradual dismantling of the notion of artist as priest, as voice that finds context and place among the hearers. The poet has been allowed to cloister his/her little self in closets and dusty drawers, therein to write secret tales about the self, only to die with them in boxes. Later they are found by others who publish them and own them—and Gerard Manley Hopkins and Emily Dickinson—what pitiable souls who had no chance to sing to their community, to truthfully bare their hearts and souls and thus become the voice of their community—their village—while still living! Thus the mechanism to assume that posture of distance and isolation is that of irony—the secret code of not being really honest—always devising a way to let the clever feel even more clever because they have understood your cleverness. We become victims of that quest. What a poet like yourself does is to reinstate the concept of the poet as a griot—as priest, not void of subjectivity and a private self but able to contain the voices of the community—virtually empowered with the gift to develop a soul for the people. It is a given art, a learned art, and an art that is purely accidental and related to circumstances.

It is this that has made me a genuine admirer of your work, and yet it is this that makes me feel for your struggle to be heard and understood. Because when you start to assume this role, the general conceptions of who or what a poet should be begin to assert themselves in a negative and debilitating manner.

Reading your poetry involved the making of a series of connections. For sheer poetic sinew and potency, I think the poem "The Afterbirth, 1931" is the finest work in the collection. This poem moved me because of the beauty of its language and because of the control, that incredible sense of control that belies a seething anger. You kept your cool without forgetting to announce the combination of abuse and insult and misguidedness on the part of those who watched the afterbirth gangrene because of assumptions. Nikky, that poem is a gem because of its complex treatment of issues of responsibility and racial injustice. It tackles the questions that many people still can't get a handle on. Who, they ask, is responsible for the woman's death? And when we roll our eyes and say, "You really have to ask that?" they grow angry or crumble and vanish in a cloud of guilt and confusion. But in this poem there is that quality of irony that is rescued by its natural occurrence in the narrative. It is never forced, never yanked and pulled into the light of day. Instead, it asserts itself as the core of the poem. The stately voice that opens the poem echoes throughout the piece, and the core tragedy, the tragic note of the piece, is locked into the tarnishing of that stateliness caused by that quest to do good and be better. Is this not the narrative of our collective histories in this diasporic world? Is this not the tale of our constant participation in the undermining of our traditions and values by a perceived sense of what is better? And where does this notion spring from if not from the plantation order that posits a series of paradigms about what is good and what is evil that really amounts to a crude experimentation with the dynamics of race: white good, black bad—work out the rest by application. And yet this self-correction, this admitting of fallibility, is wonderfully voiced in the litany of what is truly ours and what is truly valuable in who and what we are. Suddenly this tragic act, this moment of forgetting, becomes a vividly evoked Achilles' heel, a moment of complete darkness that gathers into its depth all the errors of our lives when it comes to race questions and to our dignity. Consequently, it is unimportant whether a finger points or not. The celebration of what should have been and what must be is enough—is everything. This poem, Nikky, tells me that somehow your work has to be posted for all to see. It demonstrates your ability as a storyteller and as a truth sayer:

> We were a colored clan of kinfolk
> who threw soil   not salt
> over our shoulders
> who tendered close the Bible
> who grew and passed around the almanac at night
> so we would know
> what to plant at first light
>
> . . .
>
> he left and forgot
> he left and didn't remember
> the afterbirth inside
> Carlene Godwin Finney
>
> left
>
> to clabber
> gangrene
> close down
> her place

her precious private pleasing place
to fill the house to the rafters
up past the dimpled tin roof
with a rotting smell
that stayed for nine days
that mortgaged a room
in our memories
and did not die along with her

I want to take the latter stanza and read it aloud to the world and announce that this was written by a dreadlocked woman who understands something that is deeper than a story. The craft here is eloquent. The image of the room being mortgaged off invokes issues of commerce and poverty that are so right in this poem about a people who are trying to find dignity beyond their poverty:

aware of just whose feet
walked across our tin roofs at night
we were such light sleepers
such long-distance believers

We were a family pregnant
whose water had broken
and for once
there was ham money
'bacca money
so we thought to do better by ourselves
to begin our next row
we would go and get him

Yet this idea of birthing—the image of broken water as a sign of potential prosperity—is tied to the idea of memories becoming homes—and the home is that house that begins to stink with the rotting afterbirth. The abortion of the mother is an abortion of the home and family, the proverbial womb/space of possibility. There is something larger taking place. Innocence is lost and so is the blind faith in the patterns of white society. Quite simply, a lesson is learned about breaking away from trying to "make it" on the terms set by white society. These are impossible and unnatural terms. These are terms that will only lead to greater debilitation. These are terms that are founded upon a rigid caste system. Abandoned, the room is a mortuary, the room is a shrine of the canker of many aborted beginnings in our experience. The multiple wombs, the many dark spaces invaded by this drunk alien hand form an image that will remain with me for a very long time. It is for this reason that I love this poem. It is because, despite the broken bones and the stinking death of careless actions and drunkenness, there are those last few stanzas that speak of the people who have in their hearts the truth to undermine the hurt of this moment. You name them in a litany that really pulls the griot to the fore. Above all, the complex perception of the narrator, a floating voice that is able to enter and leave old places and still speak of *us,* is a wonderful quality that is brilliantly and compellingly urgent and necessary.

All the best, Nikky Finney, and walk good, trod sof'.

Sincerely,
Kwame
South Carolina
September 11, 1993

Adapted from "Reading *Rice:* A Local Habitation and a Name," *African American Review* 31 (June 1997): 2, 269–79. Copyright © 1997 by Kwame Dawes.

My first breaths were drawn, my first words coaxed on a triangular patch of sandy land called South Carolina. This was land that Indians first inhabited and that Black folks, Africans, had made.[1] I was born to a land thick with Spanish moss and swamp, cypress and live oak, and, in its day, slavery and many a rice field.

I call South Carolina land that Black folks made because it was on the backs and knees, the minds and muscles of enslaved Africans that acres of timber-dense South Carolina were transformed into rich rice fields. Africans who by hand and horse pulled up trees and stoked back water then planted seed by the African heel-toe method did in fact "make land" out of uncut forests, as well as make European landowners incredibly and indisputably rich. Africans who were skilled agriculturalists and land engineers were cargoed to America from Senegal and The Gambia, vast rice-producing countries in their own right. As slaves they harvested the rice, threshed and winnowed the rice, and won international acclaim for the high-quality South Carolina rice known as Carolina Gold. At the same time the southern aristocracy that basked in the worldwide attention to its acclaimed crop treated these knowledgeable human beings worse than animals.

I was born in a tiny state that is half dipped in the sea, a place that in 1737 "look[ed] more like a negro country than a country settled by white people," as a Swede, Samuel Dyssli, wrote.[2] More Africans were led off the boats in South Carolina than in any other place in North America, until whites, fearing reprisals, enacted laws setting strict controls on the Black population of the state. From the early 1700s and for years beyond, in South Carolina Black people were the major import and rice its most favored export. These two entities were intimately linked. To clear the land and make it fit for rice, and to grow the rice and weigh it in by the ton, year after year, only Africans could do. Africans alone endured the daily stench, the relentless heat, the mosquito infestation, and the backbreaking labor. Whites often left the land and traveled back to Europe, unable to stand the South Carolina tropics.

When I was a girl growing up in the Palmetto State in the 1960s, there was always a punch bowl of rice on the dinner table. In my own house today, we eat rice, never tiring of it. I hold this tradition of rice culture and diet to be sacred. Rice constitutes the basic diet of over one-half the world's population. Unenhanced, alone in a bowl, with nothing for gravy or garnish, each grain fluffy and separate, rice is a complete and sustaining meal.

I believe South Carolina has disregarded much of its African heritage. The grandchildren of the Africans who first endowed the state with their labor and land making are presently being taxed off their land tracts inch by inch. This beautiful country of my birth is being turned into one-half golf course and one-half toxic dump. Its incredible natural beauty is up for sale to the highest bidder. Black people never got their *forty acres and a mule* as promised. From field order to government decree to presidential proclamation, those in power have never kept their word. But still Black people cherish the land and keep it close, still Black folk love the rice. We clearly remember it to be soil and food that our mothers and fathers made for us and we live to rightfully pass it along in the tradition.

In my ongoing passion for South Carolina, I continue to seek out all seeds of its African lineage. From the telling pen of historian Charles Joyner I read of Mary One, who refused to be beaten for allegedly having failed to complete her assigned task. "Going drownded myself," was her reply to her master. "I done my work. Fore I take a lick, rather drownded myself."[3] Mary One's resistance succeeded. Rather than lose this good-working woman her master reassigned her.

May we always resist what we know in our hearts to be wrong. May we do right and keep our word. May we know the fullness of plain rice and how simple and delicious a meal it can be with plain words. This is the steel and downy of a true life.

Nikky Finney
Lexington, Kentucky
January 1995

1. Amelia Wallace Vernon, *African-Americans at Mars Bluff, South Carolina* (Baton Rouge: Louisiana State University Press, 1993), 123.

2. Peter H. Wood, *Black Majority* (New York: Knopf, 1974), 133.

3. Charles Joyner, *Down by the Riverside* (Champaign: University of Illinois Press, 1984), 232.

ACKNOWLEDGMENTS

There have always been those on various shores pointing and blowing this raft of grainy words, as well as its navigator, out in search of a good warm sea wind. Those who have said in all kinds of ways and deeds: *Keep writing and the rest of it will come.* I have been buoyed here by Percival Everett, Gurney Norman, Peter J. Harris, Kwame Dawes, Linda J. Thomas, Opal Palmer Adisa, PJ Hamilton, Michael Brock, and Joan Hazlett of 1972.

There have been organizations that turned their ceiling fans and windmills on me as I worked. Because of their financial support I was able to have the unthinkable: time to write. They are The Kentucky Foundation for Women and The Kentucky Arts Council. It was the unconditional assistance of the Bluegrass Black Arts Consortium, The Writer's Voice of Central Kentucky, the English department at the University of Kentucky, and the Carnegie Center for Literacy and Learning in Lexington that helped this manuscript through to publication.

Abyssinian, Denise Rodgers, Lena Boxton, Ellen Sumter, Claire Prymus, Tony Riddle, Lorain Harmon, and Makeba never let me drift unanchored.

LaVon Van Williams, master artist, created in wood and paint the visual stories of Black folks' lives.

Charles Joyner and his book *Down by the Riverside,* from which various quotes were pulled, were invaluable in quilting scholarship with the southern life I know in the first person.

Bobby Finney, uncle extraordinaire, teacher of the fierce beauty of truth and pride of self.

Beulah Lenorah Davenport, I am blessed to have at my side, still grandmothering to me in the ancient ways of the plain earth, she having wondrously lived through every year of the twentieth century.

Makeda Silvera and Stephanie Martin, and the word-loving crew at Sister Vision Press, who for the past ten years have consistently thrown out their loveliest anchors to others and now to me, determined that our honest breath must live on, for posterity's sake.

The queen sea turtle herself is Opal K. C. Baker, who is where the green Halfway

Tree, Jamaican sky intersect the blue Carolina sun and make shadows dance upon the walls, and without whose editing eyes all life would be jumbled.

And the dozens of dozens of folks who for the past several years invited me to read or suggested a place where I might send work, or took the time to write a note, or did something so generous and selfless to help get the work out there again, after ten years—

Gratefully, I bow.

RICE

Handlin' the Rice

⁓

Wash de rice well in *two* waters, if you don't wash 'em,

'e will *clag* an' put 'em in a pot of well-salted boilin' water.

You mustn't hab a heavy han' like 'e was 'tata or sich,

but must stir 'em in light an' *generous* so 'e can feel de water

all t'rou. When 'e done be sure you dish 'em in a hot dish,

les 'e take a smart chill an' go flat.

—"A QUEEN OF A SANTEE KITCHEN,"
AS REPORTED BY MARY ALSTON READ SIMMS

Heel–Toe

To first dig with the heel

Drop seed

Then cover with the toe

The Blackened Alphabet

While others sleep
My black skillet sizzles
Alphabets dance and I hit the return key
On my tired   but ever-jumping eyes
I want more   I hold out for some   more
While others just now turn over
Shut down alarms
I am on   I am on
I am pencilfrying
Sweet black alphabets
In an all-night oil

Irons at Her Feet

from the coals
of her bedroom fired place
onto the tip
of my grandmother's
december winter stick

for fifteen years
hot irons traveled
into waiting flannel wraps
and were shuttled
up under covers
and in between quilts
where three babies lay shivering
in country quarter
nighttime air

hot irons
wrapped and pushed
up close
to frosting toes
irons instead of lip kisses
is what she remembers

irons instead of caramel-colored fingers
that should have swaddled shoulders
like they swaddle hoes
and quiltin' needles
and spongy cow tits

every time
i am back home
i tip into her room
tip again into her saucering cheeks
and in her half sleep
my mother reads her winters
aloud to me

her persimmon whispers are deliriously sweet
to this only daughter's ear

when you are home
she says
the irons come back
every night
i know the warm is coming

Yellow Jaundice

After the horizon
of my mother's eyes
and my father's
pinkish proudest first girl smile
I must have seen trees first

There in a semicircle
5 3 hundred year old
live oaks
drench draped
in hot august moss
in the beige sandy yard
where nothing else grew
no grass
just sand
and eventually me

5 3 hundred year old
live oaks
on racepath avenue
southern coastal
carolina
nineteen hundred and fifty-seven

When papa pulled the black valiant
all the way up to the house porch
so she wouldn't have far to walk
nor yellow-jaundiced new me
much sun to feel

I was home for the first time
riding high bone in mama's lap

Long before vertical or horizontal vision
I could see in the round
my mother's navel opening
as milky global eye

Still I love a circled-up window
still I see it round first
the bending circling trees catch me
before anything
From my first days
this madagascan nose pointed for
the atlantic-african sea
like babylips poking out
hungry for the milky nipple
I could hear calling
spitting out the ancestor crabs
from my incubating window

As I grew these other eyes
and could finally look above
and below me
after His and Her face
that I shall always know best
I surely must have high-glimpsed these ones first

5   3 hundred year old
live oaks
baobab standing
in a wide-arcing circle
a family of old wood
standing shoulder to shoulder to shoulder
at different sky heights

their feet immemorial stuck in seashell socks
in beige and white sand
where nothing else grew
but eventually me

I walk through and sleep in
that village of woody bones
the days and nights of childhood
still deeply rooted there

I hear their splintered venerable chanting
and step across the snake roots
that buckled up and ran from out of the ground
and cycloned scars around my legs
like age rings on top my skin

5   3 hundred year old live oaks

Sometimes I am still there
waiting for mother to get out of the car
pushing for her to get up   out of the car
I want to look out again
for the first time   and claim
my horizontal vision   my vertical view
and walk that village path of old trees
that stood calling for me so long
to be home for the first time

My how they must have sung
tree songs
for me
the first time she put me down
and watched me take
my first steps in that wavy ocean soil

Could she have cautioned
about the snake roots
that would   from then on   be in my way
that buckled up and ran out of the ground
all over the yard

5   3 hundred year old live oaks

Or would she simply push me from the dock
armored in a cowrie-shell ship
my pockets full of everything I would ever need
and wave me well

She did not know even then
as I stumbled back to the hamper of her arms
even as I fell into my first bruises
but rose again
to the venerable wooden cheers and chanting
my tiny lips streaming cranberry
my coming-in tooth crooked and gapped for life
my tiny face wearing one complete coat of sand
not as mask   but mussel

She did not know
as she let me fall
and watched me rise
this rising up
this falling back
this roundness
would be my life's work
first taught to me by her
last written and witnessed by wood

The Goodfellows Club

for FX Walker II

You are only kissing thirty
the younger son of near-extinct men
the likes of which
we won't never see again
the last of them kind
that rolled off the Old Man pan just so
mens I can't save
in no other way but this way

There are ones who know the difference
between everything
and just anything
who taught a son
schooled a daughter
by old grey firelight
passed from stick to smoky stick

Why they must be in their 50s by now

I know you seen 'em
but don't know if you knew
how much you was looking at

Athletes never fallen
who always played for the game
not the shiny quarter rolling towards them
on the ground
(quarterbacks couldn't sneak back then)

There was what you were expected to do
(because of what you had been given)
and there was nothing else
your work
whatever it was
was the everything about you

That's who you the last of
and times ain't changing   they gone
ain't no more where you come from

Why they must be in their 60s by now

Mens who loved poker and cards
sweet on dominos
and could pop your knuckle and their own
just kindly placing a checker
on the board
they say Joe Louis's name
like it's the sweet key to the kingdom
keep big wooden radios that don't work
covered up with a clean cloth like they do
(or might again one day)
Jack Johnson
and a crying horn breaks they water
quicker than a new blade
from their medicine chest
do their stubbly jaws

They love womens and still take themselves
a look that way
their old necks might rivercrack
into another line or two
but they wouldn't yell out
a rolled-down window
no matter how pretty the face

no matter how tight the skirt
they'd smile and keep it to themselves
or wait till Friday
when they always congregate to talk
and they'd walk away in a minute
before ever lifting a finger wrong in her face

Somethings you should still keep to yourself
Somethings are still born private

They cut hair
work with the mail
and sold their filling stations for pennies
cause Junior got into State
and needed this and that

They sell insurance and mean it flew air squadrons and remember it
love rice and gravy and meet once a year
to wear something annual
something anybody would want to polish or salute
every time they set their wooden eye on it
they congregate once a week for a trim
at the red-striped swirling pole
that still spins for them
(don't you look for them in any mall)

They call themselves Goodfellows
The Gents
Zoophead
and Sonny Boy
and slap shoulders and palms

Some still tap their pocket watches
for the correct time
they might kiss a brother's cheek
if his cheek needed to be kissed

never batting an eye
they love each other
in the loud of hazy unforgotten days

Why they must be in their 70s by now

They love a fried anything
and won't eat without bread on the table
poke they belly
and you better run for cover
cause they is all ice tea

Football on Sunday
but only after church
(they ain't the deacon
but they are the whole row)
they keep their Seventh Day shirt on all day
and somehow never get it dirty
just loosen up the collar some
to let you know they been to pray for you and back
they love their coffee black
their eggs fried right
don't leave more than one yellow tear in the skillet
if you do eggs for them
shake down bushy black trees of pepper

Short little big feet mens
big high back giant reaching up mens
with tarps and canopies for chests
steering the same car
for twenty-leven thousand years
cause they don't make 'em like they used to
and they never buy but one
and forever patch up the *best one ever*
and lean back when they drive her
like they still only two minutes old

and no   *you ain't seen nothing like it*

Deuces
Lincolns
T-Birds

And rattling Ford trucks
that all have a woman's name
and old candy bars and dusty handy fixing salve
that slide in the window
at every wide turn
and they don't marry but once
and watch yourself
when you say her sacred name

Holding on steamy men
who give their last buffalo red cent
for family
for a tradition
men who believed in making land
and keeping it to pass it on
so the children would always have something

Men who still pray so long before every meal
that the food should be cold
but it's not
they whispertalk in adult
to their infant chaps
then laugh out crazy loud
just like they can understand
and I can't

They pay for everything in cash
and keep money hidden everywhere
especially in trees they planted
a dinosaur ago

Never Owe Nobody
mine always says to me
last thing
before he falls couch asleep
I creep to cover him   promising

X is how some of them had to sign
when they called up the vote
X was all
they X everything then
just like you X'n' everything now

Ain't no more

Traveling mens
who had already come cross one water
and had to cross
have to still sail a hundred oceans more
to keep the village inside of them

Mens

Who loved the railroad
the sea and anything
that kept them and their eyes moving on
who were merchant marines
and Pullman porters
and flying JesseOwens

Why they must be in their 80s by now

You are one of their missing boys
rolling off the Old Man pan
before anyone told you to

your edges browned
and the insides just now bubbling

"Is he ready, daughter?"
"Oh he's close, he's real close now, he's almost."
The old sweet kitchen women are asking for you
and watching
so stickily I let go
I need to finish what I started

You come from them that
love the sound of church
but might not stay for all that hollering
they smoke a little
drink a little
work a lot
they congregate up under trees and talk
they stop and tip any head coverings
when any nonmember in a skirt
comes around

Mens
of the Goodfellows Club

Why they must be in their 90s by now

Mason men with pyramid angled spines
standing steadfast beside
daughters of an Eastern Star
these ones who defined a fraternity
who first wrote the traditions
when it meant what it meant
who lay their hats
in the chair beside them

like favorite company
that always goes where they go

Mens

Who can   stand still longer
than the five-minute national average
and stare at the same unmoving water all day
mud philosophers
patient as rain
who pull in a fighting fin or two
and be so satisfied
and talk about it for a hundred years
and tell a different story
every time

Mens

Whose laughter
ways
whose wondering eyes
I would bottle
but never sell
then purposely taint the milk of millions
if I could ever catch them
unready for me
but they talk
only the good talk
to each other
and stop whenever womenfolk come around

You are the last of these
always-got-a-hat-on
Black centennial poles
holding the ground
and everything standing on top of it
together
who always say No to overcoats
preferring to face the elements alone
and just as sweet as sugar thrown up in the air
in a coming-down-hard rain

Sugar
that's come down this one last time
condensed
in one dark and peanut butter sweet
Danville Brown
*missing Persian roll**

"Yes man, this one, he's done."

*Persian roll is a sweet, sticky pastry particular to a bakery in Danville, Kentucky.

Cotton Tea

In 1840, a French writer, Bouchelle, reported that the root bark was
widely used by Negro slaves in America to induce abortions.

—MICHAEL A. WEINER, *EARTH MEDICINE, EARTH FOOD*

Jordie give some to Mondie
Mondie pluck some for Lou
Lou wrap piece up for Lil
(coming on Wednesday)
Lil hand over a bag of blooming root flower to Etta
(for her three stair-step girls)
Etta go plant the res' in the windowsill
Right 'tween the spider plants
and the sun's sticky shade
all for Tad down the road
who everybody know rolled first words out last day
sundown and whose tongue been yellowin' steady
since the day of Jubilo
(her blood most already here)
just a few years away
all these ones and all they new girls
chaw on the cotton root
just for the jus-in-case
of forcing mens who answer to no god
(the evilness does so pass   pants to pants)
father to son
colored women chaw on the cotton root
until they teeth is a certain yellaw
from the top insides of they throats
to the pillows of they woman's easter nest
from the first   it is cotton root washed
and ready

Maewood African woman in a Daufuskie dark
when they birth girls
before they count her toes
(or name her)
be out in the field with her still sticky wet
pickin' the whole root stalk
right out the ground
snatching it and taking the blade to its bottom
then can it away in blue jars
just for the jus-in-case
for all the forcing there will surely be
on these here sea islands
cotton tea cain't stop no baby from being made
but cotton tea can make they babies go 'way

Harry and Jainey

Them two nesting lovebirds
was scheming the whole time
The first ever hung
in Charleston
was him and her

African spit was regular
and traditionally went unfound
It just sunk low every morning
like sweet sticky rocks
in breakfast coffee

Regular
just like Jainey
hacking up cotton balls
in every breath
and dropping twins down her row of corn

Regular just like summer come
and winter go
Like Harry with his hat
more for eyes than any head
Regular

Now arsenic
(disguised as cube sugar)
now that was a saved and holidayed
Christmas treat
like wild turkey laid out fine

Like pig killing and adding hickory
like pies all around the table
(two deep)
and flaky as lace
now that was special

So they blew the conch in the fields that day
all us what was wearing croker
had to go
had to walk down to Ashley Street
in two by fo's

to that only oak tree
in Charleston
that lightnin' looked like
it never would
just go on and hit

A live oak it was
live
with all th't nigga hair hanging
growing from
the inside out

Everytime it took one by the neck
seem like it grew another limb
then spit 'em out
by their scalpfruit
(just somethin' more for the lightnin' to miss)

An oak tree
holding on
just for
lovebirds

Hawk Harry and Dove Jainey
hanged at day
buried at night
and not nowhere near no shade
tree neither

They already had they
morning coffee
already had they shade
and they tree
was ready to go for good

Hanged at day
buried at night
so wouldn't no work
have to be missed
wasn't no holiday for burying

Hangings was regular
just like hacked-up spit stirred in coffee
hangings you was made permission to see
buryings had to wait for your leisure

On camp row at nightfall
(when the real hanging time come round)
when the real spirits come out
and spit sweet right back on the lives
of Harry and Jainey

Them two sweetie pies
climb right on off
on their sparkling own

And way up there
come black and alive with night

And way up there quiver down
on the rest of us
still locked-up hearts

well then
that's when less than what they think gets buried

that's when careful-coffee-sippers-from-now-on
try and cut the lights
and send folks on home
(wasn't nobody needing to see all that)

But folks who come and go by moon
always come and go
with or without
what buckra think
is the only life
everlasting

Understudies

I. Cara

We know too much

Nothing is impaired
And everything still works on us
Our breasts still number four
Our hair a few years still from gray
No one has pulled our insides out
Plopped us into alcohol jars
Peeled or flushed any part of us away   lucky

We can still
Run and jump and dodge
Still   we do not take kindly
To needing
Our voices dim naturally
When there's more than one in the room
If we have to ask
If it really needs doing
It gets done
Quietly finished

We know too much

Remember
Nothing is impaired
And everything still works

The kitchen
A magic shop

Holding our mother's worktables
Merely the steam from there
Brings chocolate genies around
To the doors
Of private kilns
We daughters baked in
Fingers   feet   legs   lips
Brown-n-serve till done
We fed off their knowingness

We know too much

We come
The sweet of the berry
The juice
The primary pulp

The best of toasted womens
Who lingered long in the kitchen
Who watched long
At the hot stove glass
Ten padded toothpicks touching
Their breadfruit
Their okra pies
Rising

II. Cara   Cara

We know too much

Have sat up too many nights
Trying to make it all sense out
Just to know even more by morning
Enough   to always leave the Saturday party early
Enough   to go home and cut and carve

Some teeth   some words   out
From stored vats of mama wax
Make something into something
Just to know   some come Sunday more

We have seen them
Something always wrapped around their hair
In case of hurricane
In lieu of quake
Tornadoes roost there   calmly
Waiting out some insolence
Waiting on some disrespect
Just in case it comes
Tropical storms could twist out anytime
Get loose
Through their eyes
On occasion
And claim any territory they please
When we come roun'
They settle back easylike
They know we know too much
On them nothing is impaired
And everything still works

We have heard them up
Up before anything dare move
Seen our mamas
Out early before their menfolk
Talking 'cross the fence
Pinning money to airing mattresses
Nailing rocking chairs
To a tipping porch
Saving early in their lives
What they know they'll need
Later on

III. Cara

We know what we saw
Cliffs were delivered
When our mothers ordered harbors
Sears catalogue #1269
Pristine white trucks
With their engines still running
Dropped on the back steps
Alongside
The mail   The milk

We know too much

To ever return anything
Make some use of it
Before we are anything
While we are everything
Whether we are tooth doctor
Whether word grower
We are teachers
In any world
Instructing
From any board
In Kinte intonations

In sepia equations
Teachers   come from teachers
We fall from lesson planners' legs
We stoke the air for fat arms
Toting a Webster
Or corn bread bound in code

Who learn as we go
Who always go

Back to the attic
Where the hiding is fine
Where the gathering up   great

The paint by numbers
The oil sets
Frances overlooked
Doris stepped across
No time in their lives for such foolishness
We connect their dots
We draw strong black lines
That will help us bare some pictures
Like they bore some pictures
Set in chestnut antique hand-me-down frames

We are understudies
Who have learned our own lines
And for backup
Have learned theirs too
Damn   Cara   damn

We know too much

IV. Cara

How must we go on
Do we toe the line or throw it
How far from land are we
How far from shore might it hit
If we do
How much longer is the road
And when do the potholes start
My hands hurt more these days
And your cussing is worse

Knowing what we know
Other than *their* girls
Just who are we
What will they know us for
And will anyone be able to see them through us
And when it's time
How do we move them over
Onto their backs
Push them out to sea
Without being bone struck to stone
By their bolting back eyes

Everytime they say
Come home
We know   they know
We are not coffee table daughters
Even though
The catalogue still rests there
Even though
Cordially
Daughterfully
Dutifully
We know they will open it
And   they will point   and
Will want us to look through it with them
Right to something
Somebody has told them they need
To live better   to be better
But no such better
Catalogued
Anywhere

V. Cara Cara

Until hot nights take back over
The reins from these cold ones
And the catalogues go back up with the quilts
And we can all stumble back outside with no help
Out through   the screen door
Back out with the lightning bugs
Out onto some old secondhand and abandoned floor
That juts off just like another windy cliff

Where they are the only women in town
Who preserve their chairs
Who dare cakewalk
Around and in between the squeaking boards
Streamed still
With mail   with milk
Until then
We are sentries listening out
As they spin out   for our sake

We are careful
Obediently clumsy
Girls
With shoulders naturally bent
Like seawalls
Built to hold back anything

Cara   Cara
We know too much

Even now we roll
With each other's help
Right to the delivered edge

Where we peer over
Holding hands
To keep from falling

To keep from believing
What we see there
We peep over the side
Unlike them
We know we love too hard
We stay too long
We look when we shouldn't even lean
The wall is our evidence
Long broken off fingernails
Stuck in rocks
Glimmer out at us
But we know too much
To ever jump
Where they have already been
And back

We know too much

We are impaired
We know it

My Centipeding Self

for now
without cane
I move
like an ocean of turbulent women trails
all leading south
I look behind me
as I go
and there they are
all of them
the All of me
still crossing the street
holding up more traffic
than any one young woman could
if I stop to hurry them
they will snarl the roads even more
so I keep going
stay my eyes ahead
I am 35 thundering
rainy-eyed women today
I stand still for lights
but they don't
they cross whenever
however they wish
why do I wait then
is this hesitation kin to arthritis?
I don't want to know
my feet get wet in the hydrant water
that gushes me along
it is all the way up to my thighs
I dig my toes down deeper

in this 35 feet of wet sand
that the world is slowly becoming
and the line of them
(the line of myselves)
is still crossing
I yell at them
to hurry
to get across
so that the traffic can go again
so that the people can get on
get back to their too-busy selves
but I am not yet all across
and there is nothing I can do
with any of them anymore
so nothing moves

the light changes again and again
I turn and twist
and they all stretch in the middle
but never separate
like something fingery and human
has touched the earthworm's belly
I am 35
I want to cross over
but someone in the Volkswagen
impatiently-desperately
starts to go and
all the other traffic follows her lead
I scream
but one of these women that I am
juts up her hand
for me to shut up
she knows more than me
she is at the end

I am only the head
the traffic moves again
right on through
a steady stream of Black translucent
Me's
and the spawning river
of my whole self
never stops
and I recycle this worry
and stop looking back
and marvel at all the places
where the cars have hit
and I have never run

Making Foots

Many a foot
was chopped
off an African high-grass runner
and made into
a cotton-picking
plowing peg
was burned away into
two festering sores
was beaten around
into a southern gentleman's original
club-foot design

They went for our feet first
for what we needed most
to get 'way

My papa's feet
are bad
(bad)
once under roof
his shoes are always
the first to go
a special size is needed
to fit around
ankle bones broken at birth

Sore feet
standing on freedom lines
weary feet
stomping up a southern dust-bowl march
simple feets

wanting just the chance
(just one)
to Black Gulliver jump
a Kress lunch counter
or two
and do a Zulu   Watusi   zoot-suited
step
instead of a fallen archless
wait   wait   wait
for the time to come
him wanted to put his feet up
and sip himself some

Papa, how you say you'll take that coffee?
Oh Baby, just make it black and bitter like me.

My papa's feet are bad
they beat our feet around with billy clubs
and by our raggedy feet
had hoped to drag us all away

Country corners
and city curbs is where
they hold my keepsakes
some of my brothers
who brush their I-talian skins off
on the backs
of steam-pressed
pants legs

Shoes first
they'll tell you
shoes above all else
they'll show you

If your Black foot
ever wakes you up
in the night
wanting to talk about something
aching there
under the cover
out loud
for no apparent
reason

There is reason

Lightkeeper

His pretty hand
roams to the room
even when he does not
it blindly goes its own way
without asking if it can
and further brightens
my private   just right   darkness
I hear him without a face
say what he always says
"You need more light than that."
(no matter what the state
of illumination already is)

He returns
still faceless
but with his other pretty-handed self
and reminds me once more
for good measure
"You'll go blind you know."
(no matter how convincing my argument
for the keeping of the dark)

He is the lightkeeper
he keeps the light for me
extra beams
safety deposited inside a microfold
somewhere
somewhere
hidden somewhere inside
those pretty hands

He is the lightkeeper
and it is not lost ships at sea
who pocket the beams from his surplus stock
but his one and only
bright-eyed little girl
who never knew reason
to fear any dark

In South Carolina: Where Black Schoolmarms Sleep

All around the Palmetto State
ten years before
the 2,000th
we are still
ruining the neighborhood
still depreciating the community

Mary McLeod Bethune's
school-teaching daughters
saved and bought wood
then nails
then land
just where they wanted
and hired Josh Neal
to build them a place
(where schoolteachers might sleep)
a place around other places
where schoolteachers might borrow sugar
and hand soft linen out to wind

A place where Mrs. Bethune's portrait
might sweeten up the wall
might look out the window herself
stare across the street on her own
and see them there
watching from behind their drawn curtains

She would notice them first
the very next morning
staking up the For Sale sign
instead of shaking off their welcome mats
instead of coming over with a vat of welcome lemonade

All around
the neighborhood is selling
all around
the belief
the land   the water   the air
tainted now
never to be reclaimed   never pure enough again
We can do that you know
just by walking by and smiling
our pretty milk shake brown faces
(we have tainted so many places in our time)

Places occupied
by schoolteachers
with savings accounts
(not the dreaded black plague)
by bus drivers and carpenters
with bookshelves and hope chests
and hand-whittled carvings
(not some colored meningitis)
by Campbell Soup workers
with freezers full of ham fried corn and butter bean
(not the chocolate leprosy)

Take to the air
if you must
but we fly there too

our brown ghosts know all
there is to know of flight
and travel in even more
tainted ways
than
we

Black Orion

The Star Man was Frederick J. Davenport, 1903–1992.

In his orbiting eyes we are all slaves   still
And there are more new ones of us born every day
Slavish to things we cannot do without
Slavic to whatever is new and fandangled
Polished and pearled

In his cornfield while waiting for grouse to stir
To shoot and freeze for Christmas he told me
I am leaving a world of slaves behind   Girl
So what am I really leaving
Time to go   When that's all what's left
Each of you is every letter of the wanting rainbow
No wonder you define loneliness by what you do not have
There at least   I'll be around things that ain't so beholdin'

A star man has lifted off the ground
A brilliant man is walking weightless through his own clouds

A man who did not know that things had ever changed
Because he beheld the sky as something that may shift
But was forever dependably exact
A man who did not believe that things *should* ever change
His only concern was up
His channel was the shifting sky and the always ground
He found scripture in the tissue-thin pages of the almanac
A man who did not want to know the answer to it all
Who liked it the old way just fine

In college astronomy   1959
Fred J. Davenport wrote a paper
He predicted that in ten years   more or less
A man would walk the moon
And would he be a slave too
Of course he would
If he turned around and came back here

Handing in these dreamy notions
To learned men who graded him poorly
Slaves he said of them all
As he sat before their limited eyes

Slaves would only see it as luminated soil
The star man saw it as real and therefore   walkable
His prediction missed by only weeks

This blazing unfettered man
Who spent his life staring at the sky
More than he kept up or eye on any human spheres
Knew   he scared me how he knew
Don't get on the road until Lyra lines up with Orion
Yes sir   (He knew)

Barley colored
Bespeckled
Tincaps and goobers always in his pockets
Cracked shells   his human droppings all over his land
This (this!) is the real money

At night he would stand before the sky
Arms folded and alone
A motionless dragon nostriling the dark
Breaking bread at his terrestrial table
And tossing Dr. Carver seeds as he came and went

Preaching always about the arrangement of above
And nothing else
His white corn-silk hair moving downwind
Like a cloud of gas and dust

The Black Orion
Who planted taters and melons
By the aggregates of lights and darks
By shooting stars and the aurora australis
Explained to me that I was a slave

Because I could never stay long enough
To see his meteor's shower
Because I could never come and visit him alone
There in his pine-tree galaxy
Teeming with red dust bowls and candle flies
And to his unbuttoned eyes
There   it was always too sacred and dark
Too perfect and complete
To welcome my hardbound no-count books
So many times I came up his road
A skinny empty-handed woman
And left a fat imaginative girl
With too many presents for my arms to carry

It is Sunday   I call home
I hear Mama say   *He's gone Baby*
The star man left the ground today
Lifted off without me
Just like he said he would
Gone up
Away far
From all of us   clinging sightless slaves

"God Ain't Makin' No More Land"

(quote from Mr. Abraham Jenkins, Johns Island, S.C., found in *Ain't You
Got a Right to the Tree of Life?* by Guy and Candie Carawan)

for South Carolina

Civil War Field Order No. 15
The islands from Charleston, south, the abandoned rice fields along the rivers
for thirty miles back from the sea and the county bordering the St. Johns
River and Florida are reserved and set apart for the settlement of the Negroes.

—GENERAL WILLIAM TECUMSEH SHERMAN

It ain't always so simple to fix
somethin' what's broke up so bad

The old woman leaned for me in her chair

like the time the mannish hurricane
swo swo swoon
and the blue roof shingle fly off somewheres
into the field   and spare he life   T'ank God!
and in the mornin' there go Coakley in he truck
tryin' to tack it back pretty good
this here ain't so easy as that

what I hear-tell-say he know jus' cain't compare
to when your shoe wear out
or your spectacles break
or the rice fields flood up high so
and you jus' then figure
life gone crazy mad and the Sweet Jesus
will be more merciful next year time

54

No Sa

what we's speakin' of
ain't like what glue is to paper or cement to brick
cain't even leave it for the common prayer no mo'
more like the death comin' on like a sneaky wave
cause when the land go everythin' go

if when all the sweet grass blades
gone sweep up from the field
cause the new state highway is now
competing with Queenie the Atlantic
to see whose hips is widest
we is sho' forgettin' who is who elder

      She threw the rest of her words off to the side
      and rubbed real good on the sacred blue paint
      that was brushed across every windowsill
      all up and down the old street

when the crocodile pack he mud on up
and disappear down
cause he old old swamp is now the 18th hole
and the turtle of the Kiawah
get a cool million for the sheer preservation
but the graveyard of the Gullah promise
only the bulldozer with he own security guard
jus' so   to keep us and lil' Buddy
from visitatin' with Nana on Sunday
then it jus' 'bout all gone
City man come tell me say
lessen we know somebody behind the gate
who can write us a go-through pass

She makes that same tooth-sucking sound
I tried but can't put any English spelling to

(us know somebody alright)
behind and under and all around and about
but we ground-up folks
don't write nothing down   not no more
what for   long time for now give up on words

Her eyes scan a dark and passing cloud

cause promising talk don't never never cook up no rice
now you write that down Schoolgirly
cause Geechee don't need no pass to talk with he own
and I too glad for that!

the land is going
ain't no more land like this heah land
where the brown slow-moseying folk
with their old tortoise ways
the color of stain glass glazed
been spent a life from cyan see to cyan't see
sunup to sundown
holding on to fishing nets and dropping
purpleberry babies into this heah sandy soil
jus' for to cover up with they fanning feets
like they was rice roots fixin' to grow

this heah the bought-up land free and clear
from emancipation auction
taken back by deception
they say the African in these here Carolinas
talk funny
they say we cain't understand
no developmentin'

ohhh but we do so   we understand
we hearin' is old and clean
mor' and mor' the pretty ground
say is feelin' dead today

sign everywhere you turn now
say the same
Private   Keep Off   Stay Out
and even come-for-to-see colored folk
raised up 'xactly right here come back and be
blu-blu-blu in around
playin' follow-the-little-white-ball game
on places called Plantation Cove

(tooth sound comes again)

Great Da! Money sho' will bleach a memory clean!

      The fleshy part of her fist hits the rocker
      and some of the peeling blue
      lightly falls off the window ledge
      onto the boards of the porch

they even drive by lil' Buddy   there
on the side of the road   who still by the by waitin'
for him a pass to see he Nana
him standing there barefoot embarrass them
you can see it in they jumpin'-round eye
they look 'way   wishin' he would just go on home
but I say the boy is home   they the Trespassin'

old shrimpers and dey dumplin' wives (that's me)
bob up in the creek boat
where we have spent and made a true life
four hundred a years and somebody

show up one fine day sayin' he and she gots to move on
well do tell   they might well pick us up next
slingshot us back   way far gone into the ocean too

"the moon in its head" all the grandmamas been say it
time to do somethin' for the land sake
cause right up there right now be a man on shore
with a shooting stick looking mentally (but he ain't)
popping the air up good with fear and foolishness
yelling 'bout "Dem cain't shrimp there no more!"
protesting is He water now

Her leg is twitching fast again   she looks away

Schoolgirly   when the land go everythin' go
no more muddah crab soup   no more sweet grass
basket   no more neighbor to neighbor on the porch
all night   jus' mosquito and laughter rolling out the
pearl starlight no more friendly talk on the dusty road
cause ain't no more road

even now   somebody done walk all the way up there
gripped lil' Buddy Junior by the hand
same every day the same
and lead him back to the front porch house
where they'll try and 'xplain it to him one more a'gain
it'll take time   but it'll sho' nuff be time they'll take
way on up till the candle fly come

cause when the land go Schoolgirly it all go

all us furst ones ain't dead out
for sure look at me myself and I
but all the land most gone
all us life we live by the extremacy

us the plain folk
in this heah fancy land
you keep to your fancy you heah
keeps it over there somewheres
I too glad for the sweet plain life

      Her finger flies through the air and lands
      in a bending pine's straight neck

We custom to do everythin' for weself in these old parts
Even that man of mine long day gone from heah
Done everything for heself

      Her eyes lay back and close up like a clamshell
      I don't think she wants any more company today
      I stand and smooth out my skirt
      just like I do at the end of every day we spend

No Sa wasn't no doctor for to see then or now
no store-bought nuthin' in my house in my day
we had the castor and that was all
we had the "have and guess" shelf and that was all
and all the furst ones who believed the most
and suck on root this and provision that
still ain't dead out

God still makin' more folks
but God ain't makin' no more land
course now you know what them muddy'd-up ones
use'ta tell us every night 'fore shut-eye
Plateye say a people die happy
Then they don't bother nobody
Course now Plateye plain say too   if they die mad
Well Sa

the air moves through her teeth again
it seems to settle inside her wrinkled throat
she leans back for the first real time
in all these many weeks

well then   well then   well then
you better look you out now
tell me say they'll knock you off your feet   while
you jus' plain walkin' down the road going home
that's why the old ones always tellin' the chaps
why I keeps tellin' you Schoolgirly
don't walk so high up   not soo high up
take you a dirt road then and then
and look 'round and remember
what all you see prettying up the old trees
cause might not be there Sunday week

one day
gonna be no more of this heah worration
no more this heah extremacy
one day   I be gone too
somewhere up under my own vine and fig
then   Great Da!   goodygracious then

Thresh

To deliver blows

To talk over thoroughly and vigorously

In order to reach an understanding

To separate the seed

The Afterbirth, 1931

We were a colored clan of kinfolk
who threw soil   not salt
over our shoulders
who tendered close the Bible
who grew and passed around the almanac at night
so we would know
what to plant at first light

black soil and sweet brown sorghum
from the every-morning biscuits
Mama Susan fixed
dripping and mixing
up under our fingernails
a secret salve
just like any other
living simple
and keeping to our proud selves
quite aware of night riders
quite aware of men with
politicious smiles
who walked by
cologned with kerosene and match
aware of just whose feet
walked across our tin roofs at night
we were such light sleepers
such long-distance believers

We were a family pregnant
whose water had broken
and for once
there was ham money

'bacca money
so we thought to do better by ourselves
to begin our next row
we would go and get him
because he was medically degreed in baby bringing
because he was young and white and handsome
and because of that
had been neighbor to more knowledge
there in the city
than us   way back behind
the country's proud and inferior lines

And because he came with his papers in his pocket
so convincing
so soon
after his Ivy graduation
asking us hadn't we heard
telling us times had changed
and the midwife wasn't safe anymore
even though we had all been caught
by tried and true Black grannies
who lay ax blade sharp side up
and placed the water pan underneath the bed

to cut the pain
to cool the fever

We were a pregnant clan of kinfolk
caught with water running down our legs
old family say they can remember
going to fetch him
telling him that it was time
that he should come now
but he didn't show right away
not right away

but came when he wanted
the next day
after his breakfast
but what more
could we colored country folks ever want
even if we had to watch the road all night for him
even if we had to not let her push too hard
when he finally came
he had his papers on him
something with one of those pretty shiny seals
old family say they can remember
somethin' just wasn't right
but we opened the screen for him anyway
trusting
and tendering close what the good book
had told us all our lives to do

Then we made him a path
where he put his hands up   then inside
my grandmother's womb
her precious private pleasing place
somewhere he probably didn't want to touch

Then he pulled my daddy through
somebody he probably didn't care to reach for
and from the first he pulled him wrong
and wrong
shattered his collarbone
and snapped his soft baby foot in half
and smashed the cartilage in his infant hand

Wringing
their own sunbaked arms
old-timey family
remember him well

say they knew somethin' wasn't right
as he came through the door
a day later
his breakfast digested now
somethin' just wasn't right
how he had two waters on him
one sweet   one sour mash
one trying to throw snow quilt over the other
as he   drunkenly
he with his papers on him still
stood there turning a brown baby into blue
unmagically   right before our eyes

Hope and pray
Hope and pray

Then he packed his bag and   left
with all of his official training
and gathered up gold stars   left
the Virginia land of Cumberland county
he left and forgot
he left and didn't remember
the afterbirth inside
Carlene Godwin Finney

left

to clabber
gangrene
close down
her place
her precious private pleasing place
to fill the house to the rafters
up past the dimpled tin roof
with a rotting smell

that stayed for nine days
that mortgaged a room
in our memories
and did not die along with her

We were a brown and pregnant family
and he would've remembered his schoolin'
and left his bottle
recollected his manners
and brought his right mind
had another klan called him to their bedside
he would've come right away
he would've never had liquor on his breath
if the color of my daddy's broken limbs
had matched the color of his own   but

We were a colored clan of kinfolk
who should've met him at the door
should've told him lean first into the rusty screen
made him open up his mouth and blow
breathe out right there
into all of our brown and lined-up faces
in wait of his worthiness

Then just for good measure
we should've made him blow once again
into Papa Josh's truth-telling jar
just to be sure
should've let Mama Sally
then Aunt Nanny
then lastly Aunt Mary
give him the final once-over
and hold his sterile hands
down to the firelight to check
just like she checked our own every night

before supper
before we were allowed to sit
at her very particular table

We could've let Aunt Ira clutch him by his chin
enter and leave through his eyes
just like how she came and went through us
everyday at her leisure

She would've took care to notice
as she traveled all up and through him
any shaking   any sweating
and caught his incapable belligerent incompetence
in time

Oh Jesus

We should've let Grandpop Robert
have him from the first
should've let him pick him up
by the back of his pants
and swirl him around
just like he picked us up and swirled us around
anytime he caught us lying or lazy
or being less than what we were

We should've let Grandpop
loose on him from the start
and he would've held him up
higheye to the sun
and looked straight through him
just like he held us up
and then he would have known first
like he always knew first
and brought to us

the very map of his heart
then we would have known
just what his intentions were
with our Carlene

Before we knew his name
or cared about his many degrees
before he dared reach up   then inside
our family's brown globe
while we stood there
some of us throwing good black soil
with one hand
some of us tending close
the good book with the other
believing and trusting
we were doing better
by this one
standing there

with waterfalls running
screaming whitewater rapids

down our pants legs
down our pantaloons
to our many selves

All the while
praying hard
that maybe we were wrong
(please make us wrong)
and one hundred proof
smelled the same as
isopropyl

Mary Mary Quite Contrary

July 1799. Judge Samuel McDowell in Lexington, Kentucky, set free a slave named Mary, who sued her owner claiming she was entitled to her freedom. McDowell's order contained verbatim a letter from Mary's owner relinquishing ownership of the slave, saying she wasn't worth the cost of contesting the suit.

—*LEXINGTON HERALD-LEADER*

Wonder who she thought she was   Wonder
how it wasn't raped away
a long winding memory
spoken just as fresh
as a constitutional amendment

> "Every fugitive slave who made a nuisance of himself
> to the local commander
> eventually made a figure of himself to the Congress"*

Nuisance Mary
Contrary Mary

Ranking that busy man like that
thought only queens got entitled
thought only royalty could approximate
then declare their net worth
on the spot

Wonder
who she thought
was her kin
skin-to-eye talking to him like that

*Social historian Barbara Fields, quoted in the Ken Burns documentary *The Civil War*

Wonder
what she knew she was guaranteed
Wonder
how she figured up
the total sum of her parts
and didn't bother
with the division

Wonder   Wonder   Wonderful

The Sound of Burning Hair

Osage Avenue, Philadelphia, 1985

Dropping a bomb
Is not the same
As throwing it
One can be
A nervous mistake
The other   a dead intention
So they knew when they leaned
Their ticking arms
Out their flying doors
That bullets would never be enough
That bullets could tear
And nightsticks
Could render unconsciousness
But what would debone
Tough dark meat
From nimble arrogant quick-healing joints
They knew when they threw it down
That bullets might slice a path
Through some unruly moppy untamed heads
But what would singe
Beyond skin and scalp
Under hair shafts and past regeneration

Fire could
Fire could

So by all means
Let us throw fire

So a jacklegged flame was sent
To do a human being's job
And then they inhaled
Like the humpbacks they are
And dove their regulation
Three thousand feet for cover
Leaving only fire
To lick away
Every thick-haired spirit
Within a Three Mile Island radius

Lives have been torched in a back-alley murder
And strangers doing head counts
Have trampled through our homes
Without first wiping their unsorry souls
Philadelphia is not Hiroshima
But hair on fire
Echoes the same
And straight or nappy minds
Can lift their ears
To any burning bush
And hear rats crawling away

Though fire is out
Though smoke has cleared
Though bullet-embroidered backs are buried now
It is all ways ours to decide

What shall we read to the children tonight
Can we pull it from ourselves
Do we still
See Jane
Can we still say aloud in sacred bedtime story voice
That Dick still shoots a silver toy pistol
Does Spot still run Monarch butterflies

Or do we see Spot
Chasing our Birdie
Trespass running
Up our Black woolly-headed alley
Can we see Birdie
See Birdie run
See Ramona
Screaming for Birdie to keep running
Screaming for John to make it to Afrika

Scream Ramona
Your hair
Is Fire

Dinosaur

I saw a woman
Made of limestone
Turning into man
As she walked
Saw a human female
The streets had taken
Hit and run
Left flattened and for dead
Moving up Limestone
A manly ghost
The cobblestones had taken
All of the woman
And most of the she
Out of her
Leaving her for dead
And a man
Her breasts flat
And worn
From a country's persistent sucking
A primate's nipples remained
And only that because of evolution
They say the limbs and toes we do not use
Will disappear in time

I saw a woman
Turning to stone
Turning into caveman
Pulling the last remaining ribbons
Of her little girl self
Along behind her
In a wagon with square wheels

And nothing in it
Her cheeks sunken
Like the boys
Who work the mines
Who scrape for diamonds all day
And hate the sun
For always coming up

One 'cet upon a time
I saw a woman
She was standing
Dancing with the corner
Of Short and Lime
She hadn't heard
The liquor store was closed
The whole block set for demolition
She had hard money
In her pounding fist
She had it stretched out
A withered genie with a frozen last wish
She beat the door
Like she had no feline left
And there was even a bulge in her pants
That did not belong to her

Pluck

1. to summon up one's courage; rouse one's spirits. n. the heart, liver, and lungs, esp. of an animal used for food. 2. courage or resolution in the face of difficulties. syn. bravery, fortitude, boldness, determination

It does not take courage
to watch a screaming television illuminate
another Technicolor rape of myself to myself
with a one-way screen that I cannot step inside
the action of and say
Stop. Wrong. Incorrect.

Before you look again
batten down your lashes

It isn't bravery that's required
to watch a television
hang cable around another Black defiant man
while his son coos and drools helplessly
in the hooded hands of the killer

It is not fortitudinous of them
to pay someone brown to write
then give to someone brown to say
that they lied and stole
deceived and didn't care

I refuse to watch *The Coward Show* anymore

Queen the movie was a white mammy in blackface
and my eyes shut down like solar gates
ears stepped drum major half time high

for other ground
oh no not this time
what I did for *Dynomite!* and *Julia*
I can't for Halle queen of the *Roots*

I say No
to a camera being pointed there again
at faces I long to see and cheer
faces brown and family round
Sometimes when they know we are starving
they will throw stale bread
but don't eat right then
hold out   turn away
refuse and reach for your heart   your liver   your lungs

I won't look anymore
having reached the point
even if the car is moving
rather than ride the exciting flaming roof
of something pretty
I step off and wait   free by the side of the road
past the tragic mulatto Hollywood self
and refuse to look again   at the only place on stage
where they will point a light

Before you ever look again
close your eyes

Say No

to this only way they want to know Black people
absolutely Not   to this all they want to archive
rape us before our children's growing senses
why not do on television
what is performed in somebody's metro golden dreams
so that we might keep sitting

shaking our heads
to the others in the room
to the television in the room
and do nothing
and be the fifth generation of victim

I say   Refuse

It does not take a resolute heart
to watch an electric tube iridescently portray the pain
of my slavery   of my Chicken George accepted self

I won't watch

Black women baiting white men
daring them to go back to their wives
or else close up their legs
how dare this scene be created then sent Nielsen
express to me
and how dare we look

Slavery was no opera
soaped or staged
was no historical moment
when African women conceived children
out of love for white men
African women were raped by men
who hauled them away from the auction block
like red-hot vaginas on wheels
children came forth of this violence

This is biology not Broadway

This was no love story
how dare
the illusion   the intimation of such

the sacredness   be included
be even considered
when speaking of the ownership
of one human being over another
it is incomprehensible
criminal   to watch
what money has been put on the table
and what we are paying for still

It is not a true rouse to simply throw something
at the screen when they steal another brown child
it never resolves anything to get up and leave
momentarily   because another brown foot
is about to be chopped and missing
not if you peep back through your fingers
and sit back down when it's over
it is not big of you to watch white men
keeping African women as bed warmers
bred as fancy slaves   then sold downtown
as Cheapside blacks

It is pluck to cut it
pluck to keep it off

Why not five days of Cinque the baddddass
I'm-not-taking-this-anymore African
or Gullah Jack   Griot of the Sea Islands
where is our weeklong Ida B. Wells
miniseries adventure
she of the Stop-Hanging-Our-Men-or-Else Club

Where are my brash buffalo braves that really lived
who keeps track of Black men who fly-fish in Montana
who love their mothers and keep a space for their sons
just underneath their hearts
why haven't you heard of the parachuting Triple Nickels

of the United States Army
why can't the camera point up there
that Black and far   that Black and highback

What kind of place is this
where nobody cares to see
the god   the grand   the good in me
the unsinkable in my baby brother
the golden pear in my grandpeople

Why can't a story sell
less somebody kill molest mutilate me
or make my BabyDarling buffoon fall through a roof

What kind of people
are these that control the movies
the theaters grinding out the images
that I refuse to dinner up that
can Emmy themselves up the river

These eyes are not For Sale
and have gone storm-window tight
to business as usual

Refuse   to let your heart   your liver   your lungs
sit in the milk of anybody's bowl so long
that it turns to mush

It is a meal of right and royalty
and it takes pluck to know and study the slave past
but rocket up out of the lazyboy
when they dare say it was a love story

Before you look again
batten down your lashes

and remember if it's not sacred to you
it will soon be cinema to them

Close your eyes
you don't realize
how much you are taking in
there in the dark
in the flicker of a rolling starry story
black and brown
sepia and salmon
up against a white screen
when you let them have you
for five days every night
just before sleep
then they will surely follow you to bed
and you don't know the damage
that can never be erased
that can be passed down
in utero
from such violent all-night intercourse

You are being taken
through a correspondence in
The Same Old Lies 101
and by the end of the series you have graduated
and you didn't even know you were working
on a degree

You don't feel yourself graduate
moving the tassel
from one side of the truth to the other
and their pomp has suddenly become
your circumstance

Let your brown inner iris act as shutter
when these things make you shudder
close your eyes and see
close your eyes   see
the pluck it took Garveyites
is the pluck it still takes

Queen   was a *Gone with the Wind* in blackface
a *Birth of a Nation* that needed aborting

Make a decision
draw a line in the sand
and don't cross it
stomp your foot
write a protest song
snap a photo of something real
teach a child something forever
scratch out a new picture
and sit and explain it to somebody
who might not yet understand then

Open your eyes
and   see
the pluck it took then
is the pluck it still takes

Before you watch anymore
love your eyes

The Devil Is Beating His Wife

for Noni, Vina, D'Jaris, and now Celeste;
sister, classmate, cousin, friend, and murdered wives

I go a little mad
when the sun
cannot wait its turn
and must have its way with the sky
then I know
he is beating her again
her heartbeat quickening
at just the smell of rain

I go a little mad
at all the little eyes
that witnessed
what I did not
a little crazy I go
I cannot imagine all of you
so gone from here

We are all late
(too late for Nonigirl
for Vina   for Celeste)
this poem is too late
my tears way late

Excuse me
while I go on and go
a little mad

There used to be a saying
we used to say
Glad we don't do that to each other
we left it for other
crazy mixed-up other people
we only heard about it
only shook our head
and wondered *How could . . .*

We never used to
smack each other around like this
or take a butchering knife
or a mantel clock
turn a plowing car's front end
to our wives
mother of our children
sweethearts

The sun is out   The rain's coming
and there are no more
used to be's

I go a little mad
now that you are gone away from me
a little mad
I am so gone with mad
my eyes peel steadily
without the sight of you to sweeten anymore
what I could once wipe
I now must pluck
lemons grow from out my eyes

Mommies and daddies are going mad too
in their blue-gray madness they tell me
You are not supposed to bury your children.
They are supposed to bury you.

They pick up handfuls of dirt to throw
they cannot stop their flying warnings
Sweetheart, be careful now.
You know we have to protect our girls.

They treat me as if I were endangered
hold me like this is the last time
Maybe
I watch what I eat   I smell my ice water
to be sure myself

Mother Noni's eyes catch me
in their cresting twenty-foot waves
as her last daughters stand behind her
unable to hide
I sprinkle sacred cowries
down the curve of my fourth casket in this life
and four different parts of me
are lowered six feet down
with my childhood friend

I will be her company
in case she wakes and needs someone
to brush her hair
mothers and fathers cannot watch this part
too hard
they return to the long black car
I stay
lowering myself down
into the sleeping-sister well
unafraid

This poem is too late
tears   late
anger   late
for four young women

and nine left-behind children
but not too late
for Sweety or for Sis
or for You

Every time the sun is shining
every time it rains
the devil is beating
his wife

Eskimo

Through the walls
she walks on water
old woman alone
with her winter
the sign
hung on her front door
to keep the sum of us away
says
Gone Fishin'
but I know she is there
it is Saturday
freezing
there is snow
and the thick glazed walls between us
have turned window
she sits nude
in front of her bleeding
yapping fire
her bare legs gapped wide
as a fish's mouth
already caught
hanging in the air
already she is back at the dock
and ready to be weighed
she touches down
then drops baited finger
inside the hungry mouth there
she moves past nibbling lips
(that most fish don't have)
but she is special

she has
she hooks
for the quivering tongue
(that most fish don't have)
but she is old
she has
and finds it right there
where it always is
and her head goes back
her fins rise
for speed
and the rocker squeaks
Once
she is caught on her own hook
her body turned
salmon
an old woman whale rising
through the water
lifting herself
to breathe
all the warm she can
all at once
this is her winter
this
how she cuts a hole in the ice
that surrounds
how she fishes
gets to food
but even when she catches it
the only bite she knows she'll get all day
even then
she throws it back
it lands against the wall
and the sign hung on the back door
to keep the rest of us away

rattlesnakes
and I can right now
recite it
for you
If you have to catch yourself
the catch it is
too small
to keep

Acquanetta of Hollywood

Acquanetta of Hollywood never answers doors
and jumps when she hears bells

(It might be me come knocking)
not for a baby switched at birth
but for a fleeing woman
a choice between her family
or a sidewalk star

She jumps   her fear now in its seventies
she is one side of the domino that can't add itself up
it is first the forgotten   second the unknown
that keeps her jumping
being both it might be me   come for her
and her made-for-TV-movie life

It will be me
unimpressed with reel-to-real drama

Me   with my family asking-why eyes
me with my homespun hair out
burning like a bushfire
in the marquis of the real family tree
simply my being here is giving her away

I, Black woman constable
me with her silky snowflake Blackness always kept
underneath the skin of my treasure-map palm
tattooed to the inside of my open hand

She is talking to the camera in a dream
naturally denying I am kin
I stare at her hiding inside my mother-cousin's face
a three-in-one puzzle popped in place at last
and under the camera's oath she states
she has no idea who I am   or where I have come from

Oh yes, boys, furthermore, the resemblance
is purely coincidental.

(She is right about the pure)

I am so still
(all but my bouncing Geiger twitching knee
which can never keep quiet through a family lie)
Uncle Dickman is riding it now
he and every day of his six months of hard labor
time   given for slapping a white man back
to the future   when Jesus had woolly hair and queens
came in brown   except his fist was closed and dense
as stone   hitting wild was a pretty Black man with
nothing to lose

And grandmother Bea who walked dirt roads
calling to cows as she hiked her skirt over barbed
wire   walking everywhere she needed to go
all because her Black might rub off on the public
plastic bus seats

She has caught a horsey ride with me too

I ride them all
who never had a free ride from Blackness

the brave dead of us   who did not make it even this far
who could have passed   but wouldn't dare
I think of all those
and my leg becomes a genealogical jackhammer
I have not come and brought my licorice memory
to make a scene

This is lost family   losing   and I know
she is a Butterfly McQueen with broken wings
I have come for her
ashamed at myself for even looking for the well-swept
trail with my gluey family
how-could-you   eyes

Acquanetta of Hollywood
must have imagined it
believed all these years that time would come
and she would be offered a final role
the only one she has never played

A Black woman with a family

All these years she must have heard
my knockings in the night
looked out her window to find me
there   and looked quizzically
my radar bat legs candy wrapped around
her sweet gum tree
the wizard niece still holding on   not
willing to lose   even her
even as the dream airs   she tries to kick
my gooey toes
a   loose

Hanging there in her air   line by line   alive
a Black woman   no more   no less
all of me the final revised script for her to read
the one who would not blend or go away
or accept her disappearance as normal
no matter what color of the invisible
they dressed her in

The shark child would always be me
always swimming away from the rest
and towards blood   towards the red
the good stain   Family   into the darker
water where sleep sweet
and frenzy   the air

Acquanetta of Hollywood knew
the role would be written
and the writer would come for her
she just didn't know the writer
would be me
and, too, would I subject the story

I have come for Acquanetta
with her cloisonné Blackness painted in my hands
to give back to her after all these years
of being without
to give back to make sure she has it
before she tries to die
anything but a Black woman's death

I am her living will
she cannot leave without what we both know
being handed to her on a family-heirloom plate
her oldest fear   this niece gone bad
would arrive

with script hardbound and notarized
the un-trainable daughter of some daring fancy cousin
who couldn't let bygones be bygones
and just leave the gorgeous passing auntie alone

The niece who couldn't wait and just bring flowers
along with the rest to the grave
because in a lying language
in exotic
it would read

I have no regrets

I am the niece of Acquanetta
who has followed her silky paths
from homehouse to Hollywood Bowl
who has run wild through the woods
making pecans and chestnuts fall
covering all roads that led her away
but sweeping off the only one she could always
anytime take back home

The selfish niece
they will say
has given the secret away
I who would not look askance
when they whispered
"Acquie"
as if she were the golden leopard goddess
and larger than life
and selfishly I would ask the taboo
"Is she still alive?"

Oh, yes, alive, somewhere,
she prefers the desert air but writes poetry
just like you.

Acquanetta of Hollywood
who else would search
but the ice-cream-eyed girl

Who else might take it personal
your flight from Blackness
but this the darkest one
who somersaults safe within her chocolate family tree
who else would sit in your well-lit audience
and never hold up her hand ever respectful of relation
(even the fleeing ones)
but in her own way struggle to fix the lie
from bleeding through this bloodblue roof house

No boys, not like me,
she prefers desert sand and veils
lay me bare in magnolia coconut gardenia fields.

You were not exotic
or East Indian
or jungle issue
you were southern Blackfoot and face
us and I
proud you back to that before you fled
the secret flies and lands
at your door unannounced
only so you might not die a white woman's
unprivileged death

Acquanetta of Hollywood
living somewhere with
the blonde and unsuspecting
grand Mama
is Negras
plain

Acquanetta of Hollywood is not alive
is not dead   is not who she is
she has poured everything out of
her little brown girl cup
that sacredly we each are given at birth

after all these years
of sipping bleach with a cherry through a straw
she is missing
and this is a poem for a chocolate milk carton
I won't raise my hand to ask
they would surely see the branches
of the family tree broadly grafted

I won't stand embarrassingly
at your door or sit outside the house
where you are well kept
waiting to glimpse you
me with my mother
Frances Acquanetta's bowed and boxed
starry-eyed heart
that I've carried for her to give to you
all these years
that she first offered up
in the dark of the country movie theater
high up to you
1943
in the cotton-picking seats
when you namesake
flickered and were
her real-life
Judy Garland

Acquanetta of Hollywood
the family's secret Show and Tell

but this is not espionage
nor hide-and-seek
in your pages from the desert
you write of love and flowers
all with a veiled vague face
in the colorless voice
of the exotic

Acquanetta of Hollywood
has made me painter
flinging out the dark clinging oil
to all the passing ones
that never sail or wash ashore

I Have Been Somewhere

for Kentucky

I have been somewhere
Where   they lay out poison
In the city square
For blackbirds
Simply because there are too many
And on my everyday walk
I sidestep the carcasses
Of beautiful black winged things

I have been somewhere
Where black makes their barns of burley sweeter
Where the same black
Makes their mothers' sweet-toothed mouths water
For chocolate-covered Brazil nuts
That here and there and everywhere
They lovingly know as
niggertoes

I have been
Somewhere

The Butt of the Joke

for Caryn Whoopi Goldberg Johnson

You were that little girl on stage
Made from different pieces of us all
A one-woman show
Mobile awning of melanin and goose down
Lips with a long wavy towel propped
For false dreamy hair
Wanting life to be just as blonde
And endless
Asking God and anybody else listening in on
The act for blue eyes   Please
And all the perfect moments
That naturally come along

And everybody dark laughed
It was a real scene
From many played-out
Little Black girl lives
And everybody light laughed
Cause a funny Black woman
On a well-lit stage
Fastly becoming a rising star
By remembering her real nightmares
By making fun of her
Wish-I-Mays-and-Wish-I-Mights
Wish-I-turn-out-white-tonight
Out loud
Is so funny   especially
If you already are

Now here you are again   stage right
A grown-up rich and funny woman
Who has come such a long way baby
The first Black woman
Invited to be roasted
By the Brothers of the Friary

You are not the first Black woman
To arrive at her own bonfire
Feet down instead of feet first
Not the first who was not tied up and dragged in
Screaming and kicking for help
To the occasion of her roasting

You are not the first who trusted
That these times and flames were new ones and better
Believing everything they said
You thought these would differ from those
That engulfed the corps of Black women before

You are not the first Black woman
Who walked on her own
Into the occasion of her roasting
Believing a new kind of fire would be set this time
And took your seat up front in the reserved chair
Wearing the ear chimes of the rich and famous
That could not   no matter how hard they tried
Shimmer up the illusion of blue-eyed golden tresses

You were a Black woman
Invited to the Occasion of her Roasting
Who came not wrist bound in a croker sack
And gagged with shit but willingly
Expecting cool laughter to wash you into
An even lighter hue and cry for the icing evening

Lighter   than you already felt yourself to be there
On his arm

And yet the evening was true
It proved to be exactly more than it promised
The same flames that your great mothers knew well
That licked and finally bit their skin away
At their own private roasting
Licked and nipped you all night at yours
An alabaster firestorm peeling back the skin
And leaving your white bones bare

You are not the first Black woman
Who arrived by caterer
Walked in stylishly late
To the Occasion of her Roasting
Nor will you be the last
But you were the saddest in recent memory

Enthroned there in the honor seat
While your fellow funny lover stood just above
Melting all over everything in blackface
Spitting out all the old white classics
Asking you and your plush African mouth
Not to *Nigger lip it*
As he kept rolling it out all over everything
Spinning watermelon jokes at your feet
While the flames caught your hemline
And you jumped and danced   whooped it up
Trying to miss what was coming at you
And keep your balance at the same time
As he dearly delighted the crowd
With everything from a coon's age   ago
Including the description
Of your inflamed private Black woman's parts

Comparing the overused width of your womanhood
To the sacred birthplace shores of the first continent
And the Franciscan monks of the Friary lifted
Their glasses clinking a toast the roast of you
And the vintage kerosene flowed red gold

And your white actor peers laughed
And your Black model friends laughed
Afraid they would be accused
Of not being able to take a joke
Worried they would appear to be overly sensitive
Terrified they might be recognized as Black first
Then whatever else if they didn't
No more the colorless universal-gray characters
They had worked so hard to be

They say some people with memories
Got up and left
But most stayed swallowing their nausea
Only to ask us perpetually vomiting ones later
"Can't we take a joke"
And further taking up the cause
Of blackface humor at home
By sporting more shoe-polished faces at
Private Hollywood parties
By invitation only
In support of the freedom to laugh
And in the rich tradition
Of roasting Black women in America
Hear, hear!

Can I take a joke you ask
You say comedy doesn't go by the same rules
As real life
Can I lighten up some
You wonder take a joke

I can take a joke   I can even take an insult
If I bite the insides of my cheeks long enough
Before I smell the gasoline being poured at my feet
My blood always comes to a boil   to let me know
For sure   but in order to laugh at things that aren't
Funny I would have to swallow my tongue
And I can't swallow my tongue
Just like I can't lighten this up
Fire   always leaves things naturally blacker
Than they were

I won't lose my mind in a false laughter
Because a not-so-funny white man
Is waiting for his applause
As he shovels it in your soft Black face
And you swallow in a two-step shuffle along
While he tap-dances with spikes
On an old Black woman wound
And the mothers who brought you here
Hold their faces down in their hands
Whispering *shame on you*

I can take a joke
But he slung all the old white embers
And you opened up just like he said you had
And stoved it   even smacked your lips
Even said it was good
While Black woman ears in every creek
Valley and riverbed
Had to be doused by real lovers
Who couldn't find the funny either

Instead of getting up in your mother-mother's name
And walking out with the rest of us   you sat
Smiling with his dripping shoe-polished face
Not believing you had come this Friar's Club far

And in his defense you tell us more
You even helped him write it

You   have taken on the image of the living ghost
I see you and your face is hooded
Well roasted and lightly floured
This is the powdery cameo broach of power
What it takes to make it to their top
The highest paid in Hollywood
Is a little Black girl   back on stage
With colored contacts and to-die-for   eyes
Modeling a longer towel now
For escaping Rapunzel hair
And even though I have turned my back to you
Still I reach up for the soft terry end of it
To help wipe the egg and other white things
Oscaring off your face

South Africa: When a Woman Is a Rock

They always put their hands on the women first
They do this for a living
They do it to make a point
Cutting away the heart
Leaves a hole
Big enough for bullets to crawl through

The children are prepared for school
While the ground is prepared for the children
In mourning circles the women gather
They think of a number between one and ten
Then guess aloud
Then pray they are wrong

Whose name goes here
The shoveling dirt asks
Whose tiny back fits
This bloody ground
Which infant heart is next

They strike the gentle angry women first
And when they do
They do not know
They are touching rock

Lillian Ngoyi
Albertina Sisulu
Florence Matomela

Are there
Raising the hands   the heads

Of the twenty million
Who wear coffin lines
Like bracelets
On their shoulders

Yea   Swazi
Yea   Xhosa

Yea   Venda
Yea   Zulu

All our rivers are red
And your stomping skips
Like a pebble across the Atlantic
It is family here that knows

They have more than touched
The gentle angry women
On the front lines
Where our children are illegal
Our men banished
Where land offered is no homeland
And boulders born from pebbles
Fall instead

Francina Baard
Mary Moodley
Winnie Mandela

Ain't no running to the rock
To hide your face
Cause rocks will cry out
No hiding place

Yea Swazi   Yea Xhosa
Yea Venda   Yea Zulu

The gentlest
The angriest
The women
Live beyond sea level

"A nation is not conquered
until the hearts of its women
are on the ground."*

The Ostrich

Is the shyest of birds

In South Africa
They raise them for sport
It is game
To jump the back
And ride the tough old ostrich around

In South Africa
The longest to hang
On to a long black neck
That is just shy of the finish line
That is running for its life
Wins
It is a national sport
To ride so and to laugh so
It is game to them
In their language
It is Olympic

Brown Country

I ain't turning   Redcoat in my old age
and you don't have to wonder no more
if'n I'm a fool for love
and if'n I am
does that make me country

Here somebody hold my jacket
these pretty fringes keep jumping the strings
and this here is a geetar song
that really needs to play

Why certainly I loves country
am partial to a sad sappy love song
And head back howling for a lost love
I live to the tune of hoping hopelessly
I am country
and drawn to the music of the land
not the red on the white in the blue
but the green and the amber
and the ochre-orange country

Natively black foot
with   land earth ocean
where fathers and their mothers smoldered
in the name of the Union
how come ain't no sad country songs
about Indians being holocausted
or Africans jumping the broom on Sundays
for to never see their sweetie again

When it's only me
I turn the car radio to it

the spot where God-Family-Country live
polygamously
through the silence a voice laughs asking
"You ain't really gonna listen to that are you?"
Yeah Good Buddy I'm listening
so let the chips fall where they may

Because I do
do so love the brown and the black
of the red on the white in the blue

Does loving country and craving a song
that brings my own black-balled eyes
up to the depth of my haunted-hunted heart
does that make me a country music fan
a natural for sorrow
a Charlene Pride of poetry
a Black country singer
with acoustic and eraser
plucking a nappy live wire

I   who sing along with the twanging
of the car radio
with country songs
when nobody is listening
how do you explain being African
and loving country
not the red or the white in the blue
but the green and the amber and the ochre-orange

You never explain
just let the good times roll

Carolina born
so I seen it all
from sea to shining sea island

I play it back to you
with a pencil-sharp guitar
and hambone hard with the other
I come backed by fiddle and calypso
and on certain notes
my Gullah starts to drawl

Mercy me
I'll throw my head back in a minute
even close my eyes tight when I sing
it's always something about losing my head
or making up with
or just plain wallowing in the pain of love
awwww come on now
you know how it goes

I'm no Dolly or Billy Ray
But I sho am country

And when I'm gone
please somebody feed the cat
and in return I'll make my voice
low country quiver real good
then roll out for you
you laughing but
this really ain't nothing "shakey bakey"
cause I know folks born in a holler
who scream all their life
and nobody ever writes a song about them
shouldn't that be a country's song too
or is that only poverty
the private property of bluesmen
and plumbleached women
another jurisdiction
another country

At the end of my singing
it's always so Grand Ole Opry hot
that my mascara's usually running
and by then the Breck hairspray
has wilted my locks
back down to lion-size normal
and I'm ready to unhitch my silver buckle
drop my jean skirt to the floor
and find me some indigo
to wrap back around my waist

WellShootGoodBuddy
what more do I have to do to prove it
I tell you it's true   I am a Black country singer
cause what there is for me to sing about
should   make you push your beer to the side
and take a walk through some
black family farmland some
black burial grounds
now sold and desecrated
by golf-ball signs that say   Private Drive
should   make you want to know
this singing southerner's truth
it's my job   living in this brown country
to take you inside of real live heartache
and make you tap your foot long enough
and make you smile at yourself
until you recognize your daddy's face
floating in what I'm saying
until you ask yourself
as you walk away

Does she really listen to country music
or was that just a poem

Oh why am I fooling myself
they won't never say
I ever sang a good country song
I'm the wrong shade of country
they'll just be mad
that I never let you forget (for one minute)
that country   the land   is color-coded
and that country   the music   is pretty shady too

Country
the twanging one you always hear
is sometimes sad
but always sweet
steeped in honor and family
and cheating checkered skirts
and the backside of some poor slithering creature
pummeled and stretched
into a pair of roach-killing boots
they dance to the sizzling notes that
I just lean and listen to
the long and lazy stretched-out lines
about life
but whose life
and whose country

This is not about happy endings
this music ain't concerning Cinderellas
but stepsisters and sons and pumpkins
and shoes that never fit some feet
and the lonely of life
and how to dance it back away
so why does
this Black girl's iambic feet
always have to do-si-do in your face about it
why does she have to sing country music
to herself

alone in her car to not be afraid
why can't she buy a front-row seat
and wave to Naomi Judd
singing those too close to Aretha like lines

"I love you so stinking much
that if you ever try and leave me
I'm going with you."

I love country
for the tender story
for the blazing heart
for the ache and sorrow sweetness
that is always there
for the green in the amber of the ochre-orange
in the red on the white of the blue
that I always feel

Oh what the hell
I am country   I like listening
to its sweet tang
linger like a sour apple
baked to the pipes of my roasted mouth

As I drive this back road
I take taste of it
as I pull into this honky-tonk gas station
and pump 5 dollars premium
I   sing along until
I hear my radio's same song even louder now
and look around for the twin source
rolling out a hiked-up summertime window
there in the diner next to the station
I know the words but my daddy's lips freeze
I end my harmless sing-along and look up

I fall into dozens of crawling-all-over-me eyes
that accompany the Kentucky Headhunters' tune
they are full of catfish and Budweiser and quickly
turn into razors swinging in the August air

I feel the blood gushing
cutting the music
into the red then the white   the blue of my brown

This place where the cowboy under the hat
spits the color of my mother's skin out his window
I was taught to never step inside
he knows all this and follows my every move
guzzling down his yahoo drink
he brings his buddies to the looking glass
they zip their pants
up and down like a fiddle
as one of them begins to step away
from the rest
I tap off the drizzling nozzle
I need to pay for my gas
but my swinging feet are stitched frozen
to my lips
I look away to the woods all around

My grandfather is untying himself from all the trees
he pops and stretches his many necks back into place
he steps toward me
he says I should consider history
the payment in full

country music is historical
this is the music we were lynched by
these are the hangman's songs

He Never Had It Made

These words were read upon the investiture of Ernest A. Finney Jr. as the first Black chief justice of the state of South Carolina, December 1, 1994, Columbia, S.C.

Just a plain brown paper sack boy
from a place and people
who sweet fed him everything in double doses
just in case his man-size pockets should ever
wear a hole

An ordinary brown corduroy boy
from folk who never had it made
but still managed to make
whatever they were to be from scratch

A regular little fellow
whose mother never got to bathe him or watch him grow
or even gaze him from the farmhouse window
where he loved to sit on a summertime box
of Virginia-cured daydreams
umbrellaed by the big oak tree
and in between chores
staring at the longest dirt road
the only way in or out
to Grandpop's farm
the same country road that all country boys
tried to stare down in their day
wondering what or who could ever be
at the end of all that dirt
watching it for signs of life
maybe somebody from the city might visit
some somebody from one of those shiny ready-made places

who could make magic
of a brown boy's country-fried beginnings

Maybe one of those faraway places
would take him just as homespun as he was
and grow him up to be something legal
maybe handsome
even dap debonair
and he might just become
the somebody who could easy talk
the most complicated of things
for the regulars

And for all others   be
shiny as new money

From the first he was looking to be
one of those new Black men
who came visiting from the North
to talk pretty at the State College of South Carolina
one of those kind
with the pocket chains and the shiny gray suits
with a hundred pounds of law books
under their arms
just like some kind of natural growth
stout with the law on their minds
devotees of justice
maybe he could be one of their kind

He never had it made
he only had a proud father and a circle of stubborn
arms and wiggling fingers
to keep his dying mama's promise
to raise the boy up at their sides
and not just anywhere
Don't let no strangers have him!

knowing he would never have her there
to see any of the raising herself

This one
that one there
had it sweetened and sifted
chewed up and spit back on his plate
he for sure had it prayed over
then chicken scratched around
in somebody's kitchen who loved him
through and through
over somebody's fire who pointed
first to his pant leg
and then maybe a switch
whenever he was off his daily chalk straight line

And from beneath his daddy's wagon wheels
and from up under his people's stern tutelage
he was surely begun
but it wasn't nothing guaranteed
you know the ways I mean
all silver and engraved

He might'a had it boiled up every morning
explained and preached and on Sunday gospelized
by an early rising grandmother
Then a significant Claflin College
and I'm quite sure he soda jerked it back and forth
and baked his dreams in his own high hopes
to try and make sure it could so maybe happen

The Good Lord willing and the creek don't rise

But he never had it brought out on some royal platter
never had it promised to him at his broken bones of birth
the making of this man's silk deeds

came straight from polyester dreams
from tears and seawater sweat
from love and dirt   work   and the graciousness
of his God
all following him like a North Star

He always loved the law
even in the middle of all those many years
when his own daughter argued history to him
poeting always what wasn't right   fair   or true
how he with the calm of a sailor
who had seen the ocean at its worst and then its best
with all the faith two eyes could keep safe for her
how he would always   no matter   say

The law works Girl

And his own poetry has kept what was right   right
And he has kept her   and the law breathing

A steady drop of water will wear a hole in a rock, Daughter
Such are the vicissitudes of life, Son
If you see me and the bear fighting go help the bear, my friend
It's alright, Babygirl, you win some and you lose some
Just do the best you can with what you got everybody

He is the Justice Man
and from waiting tables as a young lawyer
for the white and the privileged
to this day here   he has always believed
back then as boy with only a road
up here as man who never looks back

The law works Girl

Papa
daddy
the Justice Man

You never had it made
but here you are making it
and all of us cross over with you
proud as peacocks in our brightest polyester

Maybe that's what Pop
maybe that's what Mama Carlene
would say

Winnow

To free from the lighter particles of chaff and dirt,

Especially by throwing it into the air and allowing

The wind to blow away the impurities

The Turtle Ball

for O K C Baker

This is not a Saturday night
Not a pumping pulsating dance floor
This is Sunday
This is church
This is now

As private as a first kiss

I have asked permission
From the Old Sisters on the front pew
And am already in good favor
With the deacon board
Now   if you would only say   Yes
To slow dancing
In church   or some other
Sacred and worshipping place
(The ocean perhaps)
Then this private prom
Could at last begin

This is not some ballroom
Nor Saturday
This is a tortoise dance
This   a snail prom
So if they want
Let them say that
I have been a slowpoke with you
A good dance
A good slow dance in a sacred place

Where the lights stay dim all night
And the record is a long play
And the blue-light corner
We have spidered ourselves into
Is all night reserved
And the record spinner himself
Recently in love
Is what I'm wanting

I have already said Hello
And now I am introducing myself
As the one who would sit out all the others
And wait for a slow dance with you

In gradual two-step time
And not all in the same sudden hello breath
But while all the other songs
Go on and play
While I wait
For the right one

At first sight
There is always our hello hug
And you *don't know*
But I'm really practicing
How to lean into your arms
Really   I'm noticing
Where your hands might rest
That night at the ball
Really   I'm chalking out
Where our hips might ask each other to dance
I am imagining
How to ask for this dance of dances
From you

I am asking   you
For a good   long   slow
Deliberate turtle dance
And I am taking my time
Snailing this one
All the way out
So everytime
My hands come near
Don't know
They are
Dropping some of myself
Down inside your deepest pockets

Don't know
Of these places so far and down
That you can't check for lost coins
That you can't reach to warm your hands
It's too far and down
A place where even washer-machine water
And dryer air   leave be
Can't clean or dry
Won't wet or heat
Don't know
These deep and downy places
That have been put here

Specifically
For things
For the saving
For the savoring
For slow notes

If I take my time
If I mosey and don't gallop
To the inside island landing of your arms
There is a chance

I'll get there
If I wait until the one slow song comes on
And skip all the fast ones in between
If I hoard my breath and bank my movements
I know the slow turtle anthem will play
The one
Where your eyes are not given
But rather take
Their brown tortoise shell time
To see me
Through and through

The one where you will size me up
With a Jamaican gauge
Using increments of some secret family measure
Where no hands are allowed
Where no fingers can roam
The one where only legs can hold on
Where one pelvis becomes an altar for the other
Where arms have nothing at all to do
It might take some sweet time
But I want to get right there

A slow dance
Cannot be hurried
And can never be asked
Of just anyone
But I am asking you

Come to the center of the floor
With me and when the song is over
And my arms try talking
Try telling me
That the dance is done
But my thighs refuse them attention

I will have waited
For the slowest one
The turtle dirge
That always comes at the end
Long after
All the others
The one that lasts
The last one
A long play please mister
The one everybody realizes
And comes in close on
The one always remembered
Always reminisced

The one
Blouses run out of waists for
That one there
Where shoes
Kick themselves over into corners during
Or at the first note of
The very one
Where eyes have to be closed
Or the music will stop
Where hair of any crinkly crimpled kind
Is left flat and damp and dewy
The one that always comes on
Just before those ruining lights do
The one I want to hear
Right when I am
Sweaty and tired and ready
To go home with you

Just so
We may never get
No place
Too fast

Tenderheaded

I am
And have been
Since they used to pass me around
By my three mule braids
Like a bowl of briarberries
No one wanted to touch
But everyone wanted to see

"You take her!"
"Ohh noo ma'am, I had her last time, remember?"

Nobody
No   body
Wanted to straighten this hair
And I didn't want no body to

Cotton mud brown
And a continent thick
They made bets on what color my scalp was
And how long it would take to get there
Then they would circle all around
Hover   over the swivel chair
Just to know who had won
And who had lost
Easily
It was a day's travel
From first to last sizzling stroke

Afterwards
Whoever lost
Somebody politely walked over

And regretfully informed
The rest of her waiting customers
That she would be unavailable
For the rest of the day

While in the back room
Already   she was soaking her fingers
In a bowl of something sudsy and smooth
Readying them
For their ordeal
And for the next four hours
I was hers

By large unsympathetic fingers
She would take me
Unmercifully
From chair to sink
To chair
To dryer
Back to chair
And then finally
Lead me up front
Near the Clyburn's Beauty Shop sign
Somewhere safe and far away   from those hands
Where my scarlet and throbbing head
Where my scorched ears
Could better cool

Behind me   I could hear her
Back with her girls now
Her fingers returned to that sudsy bowl
Waiting   I suppose
For the color and the feeling to return
I could hear her
I could hear them all good
Talking and teasing

About how the Lord
Must've got me mixed up
With somebody else
Maybe even two or three people
Giving me all that hair
And tenderheaded too

Saying how some poor soul
Out on the street right now
Walking around with a big ole buffalo brush
And just a finger snap of hair
Steady pleading their mama
Or maybe even an auntie
For some squatting time inside
That sacred place of places
And once inside those gapping legs
How eyes would close up around
Hands scratching and brushing
To high heaven

How they would sit so perfectly still
While their scalp got raked and planted
Making sounds like they never wanted any of it
To stop

Still not knowing they so mismatched
Not knowing maybe I got some
Of what belongs to them

Don't know how good I can hear
Their laughter ringing off the glass
That my head has made into
My cooling board
Just like they don't know
How hard I'm trying not to hear them

How hard I'm steady peeping outside
Longing for to
Get away
Ride away
Inside the safety
Of that '69 Buick
Back beside the generous giver
Of this tenderheaded crown

Living On What

(Used to be   If we put out a call
It meant   I need you   Please come
I am putting out a call   for Carolyn Rodgers, poet.)

Stay   is what they always say without thinking
And   *live on what*   they never seem to realize
I have the need to always know
Please   speak to what is required
For staying   for whole breath
There will be no tempting   no luring in
With any found-out favorites
Pardon me as I look around

Where is that hair that does the Lindy Hop with water?
Which are the noses that throw fists back up at burly wind?

I might can wait a few more minutes longer
But   never   can I   stay

I am black molten woman
Poured out just this way
I get all over everything
That is how   I stay

Summer or winter
My coat doesn't change
I require the same
Genuine   brown touches
More than insurance or tenure
Garlic and goldenseal are good

But life supplies of both
Still incomplete me

Keep your state-of-the-art StairMasters
And give me the wicked windy climb
To the top of a lover's sooty sweet arms
Give me   I need
The soft calloused open hands of my sisters
Spotting for me
As I trip and trampoline
Each day for the truth

Used to be
In the misting night
We would go looking for each other
Do we still?
Or are we now accepting
Just what they say
That some of us
Are
And will stay
Missing forever

My species is not extinct
But we have been told
Not to look for each other anymore

With the hands she helped give
I look for the woman
Who peeled the Sunday girly gloves away
Off Black woody fingers
Twenty years ago today
As I turned the pages of her first poems
And she gave me good reason
To stay

Mae/I

"When you wear your hair like that they say you are able to speak directly with your ancestors," said a stranger to a poet in a copy shop where she worked for minimum wage.

Mae Jemison flew her maiden voyage
And now won't comb her hair

The first Black woman in space has gone up
Straightaway and come down crooked mad

Refuses to straighten up
And sometimes can be seen

Standing very curly at her window
Speaking first in Russian, Japanese, and at last Swahili

Willingly, she flew into the lunar dust
Of some others' civilization

Eagerly raised her hand precisely calculating
The particle matter of a zooming eggish star

She did all that   and more
But the mission specialist won't come back   and comb

Not another strand she promises
As she hands over *most* of what she brought back

Grandmothers say in jealous
She saw the great beyond when she was there

My astronaut says she liked the outer reaches of black
Enjoyed the dark   out-of-control spinning air

The others that went along
Returned with a picture or two

But the mission specialist
With the degree in African American studies

Who reads the world's languages
Doesn't wish to run the risk

And ever to be mistaken as a tourist
In a galaxy homeland

She has gone to the beyond
And is now her only journey left

And with all praises from hair that snaps and locks
Why   she's as out of control as her follicles

And the Wheaties box floats away
As a possibility

Out somewhere in space
Knowing it cannot have her either

Kellogg's would never be sure of
What her hair might want to do

From this day to that   Black hair on a Black head
Of a Black woman astronaut

Been to visit her sky ancestors
Is so future and unpredictable

Mae Jemison antennaed herself back to her very own
Future   somewhere on her maiden voyage line

She intersected with the African bone of the galaxy
And now wishes to be more

Than just an acquaintance of herself for the rest
Of her time on this scrambled egg of a planet

She will do her work
But will not experiment with her hair

This she knows for true
Cosmogony is an absolute curly science

There are confirmed signs   she has indeed been bitten
By something strange and lifelong

The talking seed of all the planets
Has been pinched back to her insides

By a cobalt blue woman vacationing on the moon
Who knew she was coming

And couldn't let her fly all that way
And not be made a dimpled daughter of the Dogon dust

Rosemary-oiled moons grow inside
The belly of Mae Jemison, astronaut queen

And her recently tangled eyes
Give her an oceanic view from the speckled air

That will never let her comb herself back down again
Afrolantis

Cosmogony is so high
Black and exact

It is a Black woman's science
This peppery space

Of course now   they can't let her out of their sight
Now that she won't go and comb

Now that she's forever connected
National security could never stand   to not know

What it is we curly ones
Keep saying only to each other

"Jemison . . . she's at the window again . . . I couldn't
make it all out . . . the language . . . and hair just like hers . . ."

They'll tell her she'll forever need permission
From now until   to ascend the borders of space

Mae/I   astronaut   who let her hair go back
To where her eyes had already been

To what her mind already knew
Mae/I   is granted

Love Marrow 3

In times
Of drought
And kissing famines
You
Irrigate down
Lip juice
Into my lone sole dimple
And seven stubborn chin hairs
Are the crop
That grows

I come
From a farmer's daughter
An empty well
Sits in my cheek
And in the country
No such thing
As turning sideways
Jaw to sky
Waiting to catch
Just anything
That falls

In times
Of drought
And kissing famines
You know

Exactly what you need
You know
Ain't but one store
Always open
For business

Mute

I once had a lover
With bright African sunrise eyes
Who could not hear well
And therefore could not tell
If it were train or boat
Whistle moving
Off into the distance
And would nudge me awake
Right in the night's middle
To be sure

Well?

And with my closed eyes
I would answer
Depending on the whistle's echo
And we would give ourselves
Back to sleep
Secure
That we were both right

Once I had a lover
With bright African sunset eyes
Whose hearing failed
Who walked away
Just as I whistled
As I blew
Just as my wheels made it onto track

A perfect lover
A lover perfect
With two
Deaf ears

Permittable Thunder

Up seesaws
And all the way down slides
I was told
Not to wiggle around so much
Stared still often
New warnings came along
With every inch I grew
Learn how to move
Or else be labeled frisky
Else be thought of as fresh
Careful
Not too much twisting
About in my chair
A dress is to be kept down
Legs pretzel crossed
My hands should be at my side
Or never farther
Than my lap
Where I could watch my brother
Romp and roam
Be mischievous and inquisitive
His always curious legs flying up
2 dark wings
Opening closing
At natural will
As I grew I was reminded
Bras were for keeping in

No brazen hussy lifting up
And breasts
Should bulge not bubble

Stop jiggling girl!

And make sure
Be certain
You've heard of girdles
Whether one is needed yet or not
Get familiar with the word
Before too long
My hips
Should never get there ahead of me
Or turn any boy's head on the way

Dress
So as to not entice   incite
Or bring the female wrath
Upon myself

I boarded trains
And took my quiet designated seat
On buses and at desks
Careful that my legs were properly pressed tight
Two lovely squirming golden sardines
In a tin tight girlish can
That were never too wide
(For me they are never wide enough)

On the same pew row
Right next to my brother   my father
Whose legs were always forgotten
Whose legs flapped open easily

Packaged from the first
With prefit hinges that sat flat and gapped
Like sacred male shoots
Rootstalks running down the same as mine
That took up enough space
And spread out wide enough
Those "snails and whales and puppy dog tails"
Where two of me
Could have fit
Even though I was the taller

From the waist down
We women are taught
From the same girlhoods
From the same missing paged
But still often quoted books
By the same motherwords
The same daddystares
We see the same brother scenes unfold
Over and over
Until our lives are rewind buttons
Automatically pushed in
For life
We are told even in our grown worlds
To be perfectly still

To keep perfectly quiet
And let the world
Feel on us
Tug at will
Pull at whim
Reminded only to keep it in
We decide we can do even better than that
Because as girls we have been so well taught
To always help
We help even when we are not asked

We push it even farther down
So no one will think
To call us a name
That means
We are not *nice* girls

But I am a nice girl
Who has known the rules
Memorized the warnings
Felt the restrictions

I realize the course intended for me
But know the one I'm walking instead
We are taught and told not to
But I am returning the rule
Removing the law

I have to move
More than this allotted respectable inch
Tagged at birth
More than what has ever been allowed before
I have to have all of what I come from
I need
Then want
Each of my twists and turns
My bends and bows and curtsies
Gracious but free

Like   Bajan woman
Walking across her sand
Riding her own seven hips
As if there were a trusty steed beneath her
Taking her across safely
Yet there is only her
Self

Moving without a pass
Armed only   with some other ancient permission

Like   Senegalese woman queens
Standing doing nothing
Only moving the chew stick
From one side of her mouth to the other
Before she crosses the street
That claps all around her
Like permittable thunder
That through the house curtain
That as girl
Mama showed me once
How to hide from
Or else get struck by

I reach for this kind of mortar to pestle
Movement to put on
To tighten around myself
For myself

I am this kind of torrential grinding quiver
Don't stop me
From coming
From crossing
The street or the river or the dance floor
Just like this
Don't ashame me
Or keep me from
This kind of walkflying movement
That shakes the ground good
From taking me like a golden black tongue
Through a sensuous mouth area
Between teeth and gum

Like   Guyanese woman
Suck you in all sweet like pawpaw fruit
Like   Kingston woman
Blowing you back out
Through her tamarind gap
How far   depend on the mountain
Coffee wind that day

Like   Fulani woman
Turning away from you
Disgusted with all your foolishness

Busksport Bahia woman
St. Helena Island South Carolina woman
Balancing their lives on their heads
Betting you they can make it across
By dangling an extra hand on their hip
Threading themselves into sweetgrass baskets
Akimboing one arm
Through another sister's
And walking their own paths
And be together in going home

I want all of the mango and motion
That I got coming to me
To be mine
I'll take the overtow
That accompany these lumberjack breasts
I'm taking whatever's mine
You don't have to hold it out
Just to keep me
From being called a name
I am a name
I know the movement I come from

I'm claiming the inside and out of all my bloodlines
I'm trembling right along
With the rhythm of the ground
I come from ground
And genetically I know
Sweat

I know what I own
Know what owns me
I have begun to count
Each of my undertides
So that whether I am
Underneath following
Or on top leading
Beneath directing
Or in between igniting
Welling up then running over
Any prescribed level
Whether walking ahead of you
Or dancing you around
In your sleep

I am inside
Both of us
And fully free in my frenzy to feel
All that I got coming to me
So that whether
I am sitting or walking
Balancing or counting
Dancing or staring
Crying or mending
My hair
I am bound to my own quiver cocoon

Give me all I got
Coming of myself
So that when I finally
(If ever) stop
You really know
That this time
She has truly
Come and gone

The Vertigo

for Beulah Lenorah Butler Davenport

I am one-third her years
Half her name
And our ailments match our age
But to the same well do we go
Dropping our prosperity buckets
Instead of surrendering ourselves
To all the starched Whitecoats
That wait for us to timber

We takes the goldenseal
And dip soup spoon to kerosene jug
Hers   comes from the mail order
And the barn
Mine   from the health food store
We believe and ingest
The pure root itself
Then wipe the butt of amber spoon off
On the wide charcoal slides of our throats

Hers fights off
The vertigo
And some kleptomaniac
Roaring of the inner ear
That always steals her away from me
Mine swaddles a sissy sore throat
And reddens my tomboy blood
Back strong

We are not the same
I only have half her name

I am not one cup the woman of this one
Even though many times
I have swallowed her whole
She is circa built and steam engineered
I am her salt block laid out to pasture
Waiting to be licked
By her cow milking country tongue

At her ancient unknown age
She walks her floors
Soundlessly

Holding cups of buttermilk up high
And chopping biscuits down into it
Like rice in a hand bowl
In one Asian motion
It all goes from porcelain to mouth
How does she know Cantonese
        She cannot hear my wonder

She walks her floors barefooted
And her mean snapping dogs
That bite everything that moves
But her
Melt back into puppies
How has she taught them time travel
        She cannot hear my wonder

When the vertigo comes
When the roaring steals
Their hand licks
Are all that spare her complete loneliness

And in between her singing to Calvary
She wants to know
Who moved the goldenseal
And is hers
Somewhere in my room
I hear my dresser drawer slam

The vertigo has her again

She hunts blackberries in the thicket for me
Like a man with a gun needing food
Her hands shoot desperate
Out to the bush
And back to pocket
Later they will sit up
In her July kitchen sill drying
Big as walnuts
Sweet as Jesus candy
Waiting to be mouthed
Soon she will mash them down
With the butt of her hand
That is as smooth as fresh blown buttered glass
Boil them
Three times around
Siphon off the seeds

Then hand over an airtight mason jar
Full of hazy cobalt holy water
Just for me

And I run with it up to the hayloft
And look out for snakes before I sit
But then I drink
And she runs right through me
And lilacs up my insides

She is cold and sweet
And just as blue as her hair
And I drink too fast
And try to stand
But her vertigo
Has body swapped
It has me now
And I wear her worst ailment
Willingly
Wantingly
And her cow milking country tongue
Returns
And licks

I would be just like her
If I were not already all this other

I am not one cup the woman of her
Even though
Every time
I drink her down this way
Something folds me inside out
I turn turquoise
And find myself
Set still inside her silver

At eight
I watched
Her wringing heads around
24 fryers
That were once her prized biddies
That a white man always bought
From the mail order
That over time she fed and watched
Biddies that she named and watered
And kept warm

With a 20-watt lightbulb
Like a hen with a hundred chicks
These are the heads that she wrang around
For our faceless winter means
Until they finally
Popped

"Come and watch"
She called me away from the tree
Or maybe it was the top of the shed
An amber dipper waving in her hand   again
And all around
Red hushed heads in one pile
Jerking white bodies in another
And a black boiling pot
Waiting to blanch

Afraid to go closer
I lean for her
I wonder
How can she see my swollen throat from there
I swallow slow
And she burns and runs toe down
"Put that book 'way now."

She never said *I love you*
And when I go and say it now
She touches her temple
She wobbles away
She tells me
"It's the vertigo."
It has her in another spin

"Nuh mind now . . . just nuh you mind."
That means I'm taking too long   again
That means the sun's been up

And the road'll be too hot to walk soon
She has already turned from me

"Nuh mind, Lynn Carol"
that means I'm talking too much
explaining everything   again

A sure sign
I'll always have problems in my life
Cause   I got to go and scribble it down first
Cause   I always got to remember
Where I put my watch
"By then," she says
"You could've just gone on and done it."

She has turned and is almost out of my sight
She says I always try to make it make sense
And life give you only enough time   just to do it
"Nuh mind, you."

I look up and she's gone
Way on up ahead
And the only trail
This woman with no feet prints can leave
Winds down my dry towel throat

It is a blackberry
It is a purpleberry
A salty indigo wash
Painted down
The whole wide slide
Of my inside body

I am not
One cup the woman
That I was half named for

But every time I swallow
Kerosene rises and lights
And I turn turquoise twice
A womb stone set
Inside her silver navel place

How does she know
Every little thing
I always need to know
I wonder
But it's back again
And too late to ask

The Mapmaker

for FX Walker II

We sent for
A man with hands
A carver
A stonecutter
A chiseler
Someone to dig through
All the distortions
To etch us right
Someone to bring us out
Out of all the wood grains there are
And finally be
All our living colors
Mapmaker
Your touch
And wood talks
Like a compass
Protractor
Between all your many hands
Measuring us out
Underneath all your sawdust fingernails
Rulering us around
Knowing us so
From here to there   just so
Making us
Hair that branches and breaks
Into lakes and rivers
Making us
Ears that curve back around
Like mothercountry ways home

Making us
Noses that are citystates
Eyes that are the oysterbeds of constellations
And lips   twin countries
That sit open to the sea

Here sits the shape of us
We sent for
Just a man with hands
But a mapmaker
With X in his name
Marking all our treasure spots
Has
Come

The Savoy, 1926

This was indeed one of the first places where women couples danced together and danced wickedly . . .

—ANONYMOUS BYSTANDER

Enter

The Palais de Danse
The greatest floor in the world
Harlem's Lenox Avenue
The whole block a floor
Only Saturday night
Only Sunday
After Abyssinian Baptist ceased
Its own rocking
And let the saints go change into doggin' clothes
75 cents would get you in
The rest of what you saw
Would keep you

Enter

Marble staircases
Glass chandeliers
Orange and blue the scheme
Two hundred feet long
Fifty feet wide
The floor hummingbird maple
Nailed down
Night after night
Only Saturdays
Only Sundays

With taps and polished high up heels
Hammering the hummingbird hard
Music just as sweet as August ham

Enter

Now playing
The Savoy Bearcats and the Royal Flush Orchestra
Hot Lips Page and Louis Armstrong
Duke Ellington
Chick Webb

Enter

Anybody regular
Collard green pot washers
And Model T mechanics
Negrotarians from downtown
And oh yes   businessmen
Alice Faye
Greta Garbo
And them two brown girl regulars
Name of Moss and Maggie
One a bird's eye pumpkin maple
The other a high yellow mustard seed
Always holding each other a spot
in the come-in line

Lana Turner
The Roosevelts
A Prince of Wales
Some millionaire
A playboy
A madam
The place
Savoy

And over there in the Cat's corner
Them 2 brown sweet-eyed regular ones
Ain't tryin' to fool nobody
Moss and Maggie
Two on-each-other girls
Humming a hole in the maple
Jagging the jig
While they knit a eye-lit stitch in each other
Never touching
But daring that
While they wait right there at the Cat's
Invisible rope   cheering him on
He so draped down
Jookin' in his spotlight place
A race man
A sportin' life
The rug cuttin' center was Cat's corner
The spotlight spot
Only the king of the floor danced there
Until he was navy blue in the knees
(Sail on Cat man)

and when he finally wear down
he takes his hanky out
and surrenders
but only to himself
then strolls away with a hiccup walk
to fetch him some cold cat juice
nobody ever takes over his corner
cause they say
the floor right then and there
is always too hot for anyone to follow

Nobody but them two regulars
Who never find nothin' too hot

Who broke the mold
Then glued it back
Here   they come again

Two   who drive all day and night
Two   who been waiting for him
To go on his evening stroll
Been waiting for him to thirst up
Like only he can
And then go King-winking around
Just like they been minute by minute
Wishing he would

There he go   his back is turned
And he is steady peeping the crows
Through his likkers
They scoot right over
To his still warm dancing board
And Negrotarians and ambassadors can't believe it
But Chick Daddy shouts out the go-ahead

"Work it girls, work it!"

Now   just look at 'em
Jumpin' up and skylarkin' all around
Following their kitchen made hair
They gone back home somewhere
On a closed eye highway 95 south
Free nappy but moving wicked
And saucer throwing winks back across
At each other
From one side of the Cat's corner
To the other

"Awww you cookin' now Punkin'"

One always says to the other
Don't matter which one it is

They are both Lindy Hoppers stomping
Scrounching the music back
Into the maple leaves on the floor
Who else would dare take his place
Right there in the aboriginal home of the Happy feet
Gliding and whirling
And throwing the other up past the air
And tucking their fingers
Into poking out Hottentot backsides
And catching each other
And forgetting hundreds more are around
And the music don't stop
And ain't nobody staring
Cause don't nobody care   who is catching who

This is the home of happy feet
And foots don't have no gender
This is the greatest dance floor in the world
And these are the Regulars

The Palais de Danse
A dancing place
Where Moss and Maggie
Two brown waitressing girls
Just up from Arkansas
Have poled out now
But pretty soon
Are fanning dress tails and curtsying
Pushing and pulling
Their wet peppercorn hair back down
Remembering their manners
And giving the Cat back his old hot plate corner
To his own solo applause

Moss and Maggie
Two who know
That hummingbird maple
On this night alone
Is window thrown wide awake
On some wicked girlish dance
On some brown and humming
Hoodooing to who love
Hmmmmm
Y'all better go on now and

Enter

Daguerre of Negras

A nineteenth-century ago

I will camera
What they believed
Could not be caught
So much still so uninvented then

Exactly—how many was it exactly?

I will lens back
Snap the words for you
And all pictures of the then and there
Will come
Gushing
In one wave back

I must camera
To the voices pulled to sea
Of the then and there
Flash to the millions
Of filmy gray eyes
Runny now with time
That pearl the bottom
But won't sink
And snap

As many as there were
Corn kernels or lightning bugs

And be photo taker
Daughter of the Passage

The Fortunate One
Daguerre of Negras
Who got to keep
Her tintype hands
When others lost theirs

Widowed by birth
I cannot walk beside a sea
And look out   enjoy   play   like the others
And not notice the pearls of old breath
Of the then and there
Bloating back
Around the frappe of holiday bathers

I am salted for seeing
The fortunate orphan

As many as rain

Come to snapshot the face
Of the unwilling travelers
That lay feces to face
That back then no one dared capture
On film

O fortunate ones
Of this next century
If you have come
Without camera
Snap

Whatever you have brought
If you have memory of just one thing
About us then
Snap

They will tell you it never happened
Cause proof must be in a tin plate
And where pray tell is yours

Come from under the camera's cloth and
Snap

They will tell you it couldn't have been that many
And was never for as long as you say

They will want to know
How it is you know
What you say you do
And where is your proof plate
And when exactly was it as horrific as all that
They will ask for your evidence
Might you have a photo?
And will not take your word
Other fortunate ones will join in their chorus
Can't we just forgive forget all that old stuff

Snap   snap   snap

    Lightnin' bugs

That's how many there were

    Rice seeds

    Strands of hair

There were as many as there were
As many as that
The more

The proof
That never got their picture taken

Oh so high
Can you count
Oh so high
The missing   the murdered
The married   the millions
Oh here and now
Proof
That many

Snap

Woman Holdin' Up All Deeze Folks

Whenever
they have
come
to take us by
blade   shotgunshell
rope   or induced sickness
there is always
still more
of us
to go
around
we never
run out of each other
there is always
more of ourselves
more still more
where we come
from

There is
a woman with arms
that they cannot have
that will not go
with them
that they
cannot take
there is
an armed woman

Standing
in the middle of the ocean

holding
up the sky
holding
down the ground
screaming
at all
she has seen

With one finger
she throws
some of us up
she plants
some other
of our feet
way down
in bedrock
she lets all the others
float liquid
unseen
through the air
around her
she tells them
the air is not
crowded
but to watch for the dip
of ironbirds
that come sometimes
and they do
they do

We are cover
we bedspread
the sky

Whenever
they have yanked

decided to pull us up
we send for the woman
with arms

That they cannot have
that will not go
and she pours ourselves
back down
all everywhere around
until we are
three plush pile thick

There are flying rugs
of us
everywhere
in layers we lie
all whichaway
by spatial global law
we keep
we are

Rough linen brokenjaws
and stiff cashmere
cotton eyes
in every taken-up tree
and unpoured
ocean drop
in any open space
some of us are there filling

We are
the puffed up purply air
the sweet swollen ground
layers of floating fabric
sheets of keeping hands and feet
ridin' clouds

like camels
we bedspread the sky
we never run
out of each other
there is always
more where we come from
we keep the world
fat
and
dandy

Rule Number One

If you send me here again you
Send me back the same you

Can change my clothes
Only leave me in the right realm makes

No never mind to me
Which shade you decide upon just

Be sure and return me
As one whole

To a Black woman's curly life
Nothing else   nothing

Jus' something 'bout the way we do
The do   the words we use

The care we take   the shit we shake   off
The porch how it becomes our office

The love cover we always find to throw
No matter how wide the waters roll

How we hide our heavy hearts
And laugh with our soup bone bony selves

And boil some water and offer even you some
Supper has always been on us

If you decide (for whatever reason)
I should do this again you

You send me back here the same you hear
I want old familiar ordinary skin stretched

On any new bones
You are readying for me

Return me only
To a Black woman's curly conjured life

The End of It

I fall to bed
With razor sharp pencils
Still balanced on my ear
Bowing at the feet of sleep
Arrogantly
And adorned
As if
I always have something to say
Sometimes
It falls off all
Cowboyishly
And hides itself away
Up under night
And cover
Sometimes
It hangs on
Nicks and licks
The reins of my ear
As if I were sugarcubed
And it a reptilian tongue
No matter
How I toss
Or where I turn
It rides my brown lobe
All night
Like a Buffalo Soldier
And is still there
When I blindly go
To wash my morning face

One black lead toe
Pointing back
In the mirror
As if it has something more
It would like to say

A Woman with Keys

I am a woman with keys
Without a door
My wide-angle perfect size
Still I pass through
And the space is made
To fit

My spaceship hands
This waterfall of feet
These ship-size eyes
A gun
The very air
It shapes to me
Keys jingle
And fish fly protectively
Around my waist

I am a woman with keys
And all the doors are nailed
Dented shut with hammers
Unlikely to ever open on their own
But I am a key woman
I come jingling
And there is a ringing in my ear
That is not song
But how I enter
I am quilted down
With eyes and scale
This is jewelry on my belt
From the living behind us
I enter   then I knock

I am a woman with keys
And this long middle sash of sorrow
Stays tightly tied
And is given to the yellow chicken wind
For whipping
Do you hear that jingle?
As I go slow
I am a woman with keys
The mother-mother of memory
I come to go
As I please
You know I have been here
By the sound of locks
Swinging free
From Zanzibar to Daufuskie to alligator swamp
All along the ocean's floor
There are attics
And storm cellars of hearts
Castanetting for a key
A black cobblestone of family
Has never held its breath

Tell them I am on my way

I am a woman with keys
Unlocking all the buildings
That now belong
To me

The Rice

Heel Toe
Heel Toe
Heel Toe

Who will douse the fire
I am spreading
And the one
They will want to light
Just because I have been here
The one to scorch me
From going
Further
Is there something beyond?

When I am gone and they realize
They don't have to hear
All this other anymore
Who will bronco buck the clouds and care
As   alphabetically
I go up in smoke

Who   has not let me go in one ear
And out the other
Which hand won't shake when it unlocks
The trunk
Where I've saved myself for life
On another planet
Where being buffalo and Black is required

(A prerequisite for air)

Let me go
Let me   go
Let me   go

And when I do
Don't grab for nervous slippery buckets
Reach in and
Just throw the rice

Swing it good and far
So that it touches ground but never lands
Throw the rice

Who will catch me?
And plant me back in mosquito-colored water
That waits on me

Throw seed
Throw seed

When you throw me away
You just throwing the good seed

Toe   Heel
Heel   Toe

Oh ain't I got a right
Ain't I got rights
*To the tree of life**

If I plant my right
Right now
Won't daughter have a right?
Won't son?

*Traditional Negro spiritual

Won't daughter and son?
Won't they have a right to the tree?

If their fingers flame
At the wheeze of their own breath
And they wait to watch all of me burn
You just throw the rice

If they come at night
And want to take
The last stacks of me from you
From off the kitchen table
Throw the rice
The rice must be thrown

Who will throw the shower of the sweet rice
As they take my work out with the garbage
As I go back
To say my vowels to the soil

Heel Toe
Heel   Toe

It is the sweet rice you throw away
But food for the hungry that will return

Great Da!

PHOTOGRAPHS

Also by Nikky Finney

The Ringing Ear: Black Poets Lean South (edited anthology)

Heartwood (short-story collection)

On Wings Made of Gauze

The World Is Round

Head Off & Split